STRATEGIC AIRPOWER ELEMENTS IN INTERWAR
GERMAN AIR FORCE DOCTRINE

A thesis presented to the Faculty of the U.S. Army
Command and General Staff College in partial
fulfillment of the requirements for the
degree

MASTER OF MILITARY ART AND SCIENCE
MILITARY HISTORY

by

WILLIAM R. MUSCHA, LCDR, USN
B.S., United States Naval Academy, Annapolis, Maryland, 1987
M.A.S., Embry-Riddle Aeronautical University, Daytona Beach, Florida, 1996

Fort Leavenworth, Kansas
2001

i

MASTER OF MILITARY ART AND SCIENCE

THESIS APPROVAL PAGE

Name of Candidate: Lieutenant Commander William R. Muscha

Thesis Title: Strategic Airpower Elements in Interwar German Air Force Doctrine.

Approved by:

_____, Thesis Committee Chair
Christopher R. Gabel, Ph.D.

_____, Member
CDR John T. Kuehn, M.S.S.E.

_____, Member
Major Robert J. Dague, M.S.

Accepted this 1st day of June 2001 by:

_____, Director, Graduate Degree Programs
Philip J. Brookes, Ph.D.

The opinions and conclusions expressed herein are those of the student author and do not necessarily represent the views of the U.S. Army Command and General Staff College or any other governmental agency. (References to this study should include the foregoing statement.)

ABSTRACT

STRATEGIC AIRPOWER ELEMENTS IN INTERWAR GERMAN AIR FORCE DOCTRINE, by LCDR William R. Muscha, 96 pages.

Germany reestablished its air force during the last half of the interwar period of 1919 to 1939, a period in which airpower theorists attempted to merge the new technology of aviation with traditional roles of the military. The Royal Air Force adopted the offensive use of airpower to attack enemy sources power as its primary mission and focused on defeating the enemy nation. Great Britain's national strategic situation, its lessons from World War I, and its air leadership all contributed toward this adoption. The German situation was different. Its lessons from World War I, its traditional views on the roles of its army, its strategic situation, and its fragmented air leadership contributed toward its adoption of an air doctrine that focused on defeating enemy military forces, not enemy sources of power. The Treaty of Versailles also restricted the size of its military and the kinds of aircraft it could build, affecting its air force's mission. This thesis addresses the development of a new technology and its adoption as either a doctrinal evolution or revolution. It also addresses the question of why one nation might see more value in strategic air doctrine rather than a doctrine focused on the enemy's military.

TABLE OF CONTENTS

ABBREVIATIONS

CAS   Chief of the Air Staff (Great Britain)

OKW Oberkommando der Wehrmacht

RAF   Royal Air Force

RLM   Reich Air ministry (Germany).

RWM Reich War ministry (Germany).

CHAPTER 1

INTRODUCTION

Germany rebuilt its air force during the interwar years from a position of near total disarmament after World War I to perhaps the most combat ready air force in the world at the onset of World War II. During this time airpower theorists attempted to adapt airpower using contemporary technology. World War I had provided a glimpse at many of the capabilities aircraft made available to the militaries of the world. It had also challenged the existing doctrines favored by military and naval strategists. German leaders and strategists had the opportunity to study contemporary theorists and to use German military experience to design the Luftwaffe and its role within the German military. They applied this study to the lessons Germany learned in World War I and traditional military strategic concerns to evolve an air arm different in many ways from the Royal Air Force (RAF) of Great Britain.

This study examines the elements of contemporary strategic airpower doctrine the German Air Force adopted during the interwar period, and why they were different from those adopted by the RAF, another European air arm. The ways leadership, geography, traditional military experience, and technological capabilities and resources affected its evolution will also be examined.

Several factors influenced the doctrinal development within the German Air Force, the Luftwaffe, prior to World War II. During World War I, the Germans had executed an early form of strategic air warfare against Great Britain using *Zeppelin* airships and *Gotha* bombers, developing experience conducting long-range bombing attacks. German military aviation developed excellent tactical capabilities. The German army had also demonstrated an improved capability of conducting maneuver warfare at the end of World War I.

After World War I, its participants studied the war's lessons and struggled to apply them to their military doctrine and force structure. Many military theorists thought the emergence of the aircraft as a weapon was one aspect of a revolution in military affairs. Maneuverability on the battlefield in the form of armor and motorized units was another emerging capability. A universal dread of revisiting the trench warfare of Flanders was ever present in the struggle to adapt new technology to military doctrine.

Airpower advocates like Giulio Douhet advocated the use of airpower as a tool to avoid trench warfare and dramatically shorten wars. Aircraft would attack an enemy's sources of strength, namely its population centers to force the enemy to sue for peace. The key was to destroy the enemy's will to fight. Great Britain's RAF was a strong proponent of using strategic airpower to avoid another major ground war. Air Marshal Hugh Trenchard was a major advocate for the role of strategic bombing. In the United States, Brigadier General Billy Mitchell was another strong airpower advocate.

During the 1920s and 1930s, as the German military secretly rebuilt its air capability, its military leaders sanctioned the study of aviation's place within its overall military strategy. German airpower advocates had the ability to study Douhet's theories, as well as to follow developments in Great Britain and the United States while waiting for an opportunity to develop these theories with a viable force structure.

This thesis will analyze the elements of contemporary strategic airpower German Air Force adopted during the interwar period, and why they differed from those the RAF adopted. The part played by organizational leadership will be examined. How the Germans adopted the lessons they learned from the recent military experience in World War I will also be studied. The part played by the geography of Central Europe in the airpower doctrine adopted by the Luftwaffe is another factor. The technological capabilities and resources of a burgeoning aviation industry and its influence on the use of airpower in the military strategy of Germany also played a role in shaping its air strategy by constraining its means.

Strategic airpower is the general theme of this thesis. It has been loosely defined as the use of airpower to attack an enemy's source of power or strength in order to directly force the enemy to capitulate rather than through the defeat of his fielded forces. Giulio Douhet, one of the principal airpower theorists, saw strategic airpower as the use of military aviation to attack the enemy's industry and centers of population to shatter civilian morale and break the will of the enemy. Air Marshal Hugh Trenchard defined strategic airpower similarly, although he concentrated on the attack on enemy industrial and communication centers. Both Douhet and Trenchard pictured the air force breaking the will of the enemy independent of the other services.

The German Air Force had a broader, more joint, definition of strategic airpower. The term "*Operativer Luftkrieg*" referred to an air force striking an enemy's sources of military, economic and moral strength to achieve a strategic decision together with the other services. Although the German understanding of the use of strategic airpower is similar, the acknowledgment of the utility of other services is an important distinction.[1]

Comparably, today's United States Air Force defines strategic attack as operations intended to defeat the enemy's will to fight or ability to wage war by striking at the enemy's centers of gravity, or the sources from which the enemy derives its freedom of actions, strength, or will to fight. Strategic attack may include operations from the land and naval components.[2]

Generally speaking, the alternative to strategic airpower is tactical airpower. Tactical uses of airpower are designed to directly affect the surface battle. "Close air support" involves the use of airpower against the enemy as well as requiring close coordination with friendly ground troops. "Interdiction" is the use of airpower against the movement of personnel and material to and from the battlefield.[3]

3

The US military defines doctrine as the "fundamental principles by which the military forces or elements thereof guide their actions in support of national objectives. It is authoritative but requires judgment in application."[4] Doctrine can also be a conceptual framework and general guide for the services to follow in specific situations.[5] The German view of doctrine in the interwar years was more indicative of a conceptual framework than a set of formulas or principles.[6] Doctrine is normally based on theory, historical experience and the technology available to the service. The types of weapons a particular military has may be indicative of the type of doctrine it uses. A strategic airpower doctrine would prescribe the use of aircraft to attack an enemy in order to achieve strategic results.

This study used English language material. Some translations of primary sources were used, aiding the study of German doctrine. Material published by former Luftwaffe and RAF officers was helpful in understanding the doctrinal mind-set of air leaders. Interviews and testimony of German leaders during the Nuremberg trials were also helpful, but allowance had to be made for the differing motivations of individuals on trial for war crimes.

This study will cover the development of German strategic air doctrine from 1919 to 1939. The use of German strategic airpower in World War I will be discussed only to show the precedent for subsequent strategic air theory and the source of lessons learned by Germany. Luftwaffe operations during World War II will be mentioned to show any continuity with doctrine. The intent is not to evaluate the effectiveness of German strategic air doctrine but to analyze its development. Other uses of airpower within the Luftwaffe will be covered as a point of reference to strategic airpower, but not extensively. The development of the RAF strategic air doctrine will be used to compare to the Luftwaffe's development, but the RAF will not be studied as extensively. The United States Army Air Corps will be referred to as it affected or served as a model to Germany, but its development will not be studied in depth.

The study of German Air Force doctrine is interesting to the modern reader for several reasons. Like other air forces of the period, the Germans were attempting to come to grips with rapid advancements of aviation, electronics, and weapons technology. The major militaries of the period had just ended a war in which massive casualties were sustained in a static battlefield. The character of the next major conflict was unknown. Defense appeared dominant during most of World War I, with offense showing some dominance at the beginning and end of the war.

Some theorists saw an impending revolution in military affairs brought on by the aircraft. The aircraft could cause the demise of ground conflict, though to the detriment of civilian industry and population centers. The static, defensive battlefield of World War I was to be avoided by any means possible. Other theorists saw the aircraft as an enhancement to the forces already existing, causing an evolution to existing doctrine. Ground forces had made technological advances in their own right during the war, and airpower had proven to be a very effective enhancement to the ground forces.

A related theoretical conflict is that between the use of tactical and strategic airpower. Strategic airpower implies the use of airpower to decisively bring about the collapse of the enemy, with or without the use of other military components. Tactical airpower implies the use of air assets to affect the outcome of the surface battle. It is understood that air assets can be used in either strategic or tactical manners. Strategic targets are generally located significantly beyond the battlefield, although in some theaters of conflict the distance from a protagonist's air bases may not be considerable. Airpower theorists also viewed strategic airpower as the domain of an independent air force, and tactical airpower as liable to become a subset of the army or navy.

The German air theorists had had the opportunity to study at length airpower theorists from the major European air forces, as well as those of the United States. Free from an established doctrine and force structure, the Luftwaffe was potentially able to adopt the most applicable aspects of airpower doctrine, test them, and use them in its initial operations against Poland to start World War II.

This thesis will examine the development of German strategic airpower doctrine commencing with the end of World War I. The factors affecting its development, including people, expected military strategies, and interpretation of past military experiences threats will be identified. The place of strategic airpower doctrine within the Luftwaffe at the beginning of World War II will be delineated. The significant factors enabling the Luftwaffe to adopt an airpower doctrine, specifically strategic airpower, different from that of the RAF will be identified. Many of these same factors are present in any organization struggling to develop a proper doctrine in an environment of rapidly changing technology. Through answering these questions, this thesis will attempt to show whether German military leadership viewed advances in aviation technology as a revolution or evolution in warfare. The question of whether Germany developed an air force doctrine with a strategic focus will also be answered.

The development of the airpower doctrine within the German Air Force will be evaluated along several lines. Lessons from World War I and how they affected the adoption of a particular air warfare doctrine will be covered. These lessons will be from ground and air warfare. Geography and military tradition will be examined. Resources as they affect the ability to implement strategic air doctrine will be covered. Organizational influences on the adoption of a particular kind of air doctrine will be studied. The leadership of both the Luftwaffe and RAF will be examined for influences on air doctrine. The doctrine of the Luftwaffe will be summarized for various periods between World Wars I and II.

The Luftwaffe's adoption of its air doctrine will be compared and contrasted with that of the RAF. Differences between the strategic situations of each nation will be pointed out, but the RAF will be used as a control against which the Luftwaffe will be measured. The intention is not to indicate that the RAF might have developed the correct air doctrine, rather to use it as a point of comparison.

1   7

---

[1]Richard Muller, *The German Air War in Russia* (Baltimore, MD: The Nautical & Aviation Publishing Company of America, 1992), 11.

[2]U.S. Air Force, Air Force Doctrine Document 1, *Air Force Basic Doctrine* (Washington, DC: Government Printing Officer, September 1997), 51-53, 85.

[3]David R. Mets, *The Air Campaign: John Warden and the Classic Airpower Theorists* (Maxwell Air Force Base, AL: Air University Press, 1999), 7-8.

[4]Chairman of the Joint Chiefs of Staff, Joint Pub 1-02, *Department of Defense Dictionary of Military and Associated Terms* (Washington DC: US Government Printing Office, 23 March 1994, amended 6 April 1999), 140.

[5]Robert C. Ehrhart, "Some Thoughts on Air Force Doctrine," *Air University Review* 31, no. 3 (1980): 30-31.

[6]James S. Corum, *The Roots of Blitzkrieg: Hans von Seeckt and German Military Reform* (Lawrence, KS: The University Press of Kansas, 1992), xiv-xv.

7

CHAPTER 2

BACKGROUND

Doctrine in essence, is a set of fundamental beliefs regarding the best ways to fight wars
and conduct campaigns. Doctrine is based on both theory and practice.[1]

Phillip S. Meilinger, "Trenchard and 'Morale Bombing': The Evolution of Royal Air
Force Doctrine Before World War II"

Practice in airpower application during World War I was limited, so theory would play a

significant part when a nation's air force leadership attempted to develop doctrine following the

war. The intent of this chapter will be to discuss three preeminent airpower theorists during the

interwar period and analyze their impact upon German military thought and analysis. The

chapter will also examine whether they were studied or discussed in Germany and any reactions

to their theories.

Giulio Douhet

Giulio Douhet was one of the most prominent and oft-quoted airpower theorists. He was

originally an Italian artillery officer, commissioned in 1882. He commanded one of the first army

air units and by 1915 had developed many of his ideas on the use of aircraft. After the Italian

army was engaged in a stalemate with the Austrian army, he publicly called for a massive bomber

force to break the morale of the Austrian people. He was court-martialed after publicly criticizing

the Italian leadership and spent one year in jail. Douhet was later released and headed the Italian

Central Aeronautical Bureau in 1918. In 1921 he was promoted to General and published

Command of the Air, his best-known work. Throughout his career, he advocated the adoption of

technology by the military and a unified command structure for a nation's military, specifically,

Italy's.[2]

Douhet believed the character of war was evolving. Total warfare was the way of the

future. A nation engaged in war would be committing its entire population and resources toward

8

the accomplishment of its strategic objectives.[3] Aviation was an integral part of this evolution in warfare. Douhet believed the aircraft fundamentally altered the nature of warfare and could have a decisive effect on the surface battle. He had very specific ideas on the character, function, and composition of an air force.[4]

Douhet adhered to two major assumptions. First, aircraft are instruments of offense with incomparable potential. He foresaw no effective defense against aircraft. Second, bombardment of population centers will shatter civilian morale. Shattered civilian morale would lead to loss of the enemy's will to fight. Using aircraft to bomb population centers could bring about the end to a conflict so swiftly that surface forces would not have to invade the enemy's territory.[5]

Purpose of an Air Force

As a basis to his airpower theory, Douhet believed the defensive was dominant in ground warfare due to technical advances in weaponry. The use of the machine gun and other advances in weaponry had dramatically improved the defensive efficiency of soldiers while increasing the cost of offensive operations. Even though Douhet felt the defense was dominant in ground warfare, he still felt the offense was the key to overall victory.[6]

Douhet believed a prerequisite to ensuring an adequate national defense was the ability to conquer the command of the air in case of war.[7] This command of the air would be used to carry the offensive to the enemy. Airpower was to be the offensive that would win the war decisively in lieu of a ground offensive.

Priorities of Airpower

The primary objective of an aerial campaign should be the enemy's industries and population centers. These targets may be far from where the surface armies could be fighting each other. Military installations were not the primary targets for an air force. An enemy's air force should not be attacked though air combat. The enemy air force was to be defeated by attacking the factories that produced its equipment and supplies and its ground installations.[8]

9

Air forces were by no means to be defensive forces. Douhet writes:

> We may have already seen that the fundamental concept governing aerial warfare is to be resigned to the damage the enemy may inflict upon us, while utilizing every means at our disposal to inflict even heavier damage upon him. An Independent Air Force must therefore be completely free of any preoccupation with the actions of the enemy force. Its sole concern should be to do the enemy the greatest possible amount of surface damage in the shortest possible time, which depends upon the available air forces and the choice of targets.[9]

Surface forces were to assume defensive roles to hold the enemy surface forces at the common frontier. Douhet envisioned the Italian army using the terrain and defensive dominance to prevent enemy invasion through the northern Italian alpine passes. Armies were to concentrate on preventing the enemy from seizing friendly communications, industries, and air force installations. Ground forces were to support the air offensive by preserving its bases and means of sustainment while the air forces paralyzed the enemy's ability to maintain an army and destroyed the enemy population's will to resist.[10] To transfer his theory to another nation would require the assumption that that nation has a defined natural frontier.

Proposed Air Force Composition

Douhet placed an extremely high priority on the air offensive. He feared that using aircraft in the role of defense diminished the strength of the offensive. A "battle plane" capable of the bombardment role and conducting its own defense was the only aircraft Douhet advocated. He did not see the need to use aircraft for air defense. A nation should endure air attacks in the interest of providing a stronger air attack on the enemy's population.[11]

Impact on Germany

Douhet's book was translated into German in 1935, but many of his writings were translated as early as 1929.[12] His main work, *Command of the Air*, was published in Germany as *Luftherrschaft*. German analysts led by airpower theorist and historian Herhudt von Rohden studied his works critically. They thought his theories had narrow application, being most applicable to his home country of Italy, which had more defined natural frontiers than Germany.

They did agree with Douhet's thesis that a nation needed to gain air dominance in order to gain significant military successes. They also felt Douhet's ideas were part of the military doctrine of all contemporary air forces and that his writings had paved the way for independent air forces.[13]

Adolf Hitler read Douhet's theories and referred to them when he directed the building of a bomber-heavy air force.[14] Goering also accepted Douhet's theories, primarily his emphasis on the offensive use of airpower.[15] Werner Baumbach, who was "General of the Bombers," senior bomber pilot in the Luftwaffe during the latter part of World War II, recognized the influence Douhet's writings had on General Walther Wever, one of the first leaders of the Luftwaffe. He acknowledged General Wever's agreement with Douhet that modern war would be total and airpower must play a part in reducing the enemy's will through attacking its industry and communications.[16] During rearmament, Germany paid attention first to fighters, but bombers were of primary importance not long after. Strategic bombers were given primary importance. In 1939, bomber and Stuka *gruppen*, numbering about 27 to 31 aircraft each, outnumbered fighter *gruppen*, with 40 aircraft each, by a ratio of 39 to 13.[17] The Luftwaffe's force structure shows the emphasis it gave to the offensive use of airpower.

Air Marshal Hugh Trenchard

Germany conducted the first strategic bombing campaign against Great Britain from 1915 to 1917. These raids caused more psychological damage than military, creating great fear in the population and government. This fear was the main reason the British government formed the RAF as a separate service on 1 April 1918. Hugh Trenchard, then a major general, was appointed the first Chief of the Air Staff (CAS). A month later, he was appointed leader of the Independent Air Force in France with the mission of conducting bombing attacks on German installations and cities behind the battlefront.[18]

Trenchard, similar to other British airmen, viewed the object of war as forcing one's will upon the enemy by breaking his capability to fight or his will. He focused on the latter.

11

Trenchard wanted to use the airplane's capabilities to forge a strategic weapon to shatter the enemy's will. His ideas were also shaped by the tradition of British economic warfare. The foundation of his theory was that military aviation should be used in a strategic role to destroy the morale of an enemy nation, by attacking enemy industry and destroying the morale of enemy factory workers.[19]

Trenchard operated under several assumptions. Successful military operations require air superiority. He was convinced that bomber forces would always reach their objective without escort. Civilian morale was fragile, but British morale was more resilient than German. The offensive form of warfare was stronger than the defensive. The problems inherent in executing a bombing campaign such as night navigation, target acquisition, and bombing accuracy were solvable.[20] These assumptions were behind his objective of forming the RAF into a largely strategic air force. Like other airpower theorists, he did not foresee the changes radar would bring to air warfare, solving the problem of concentration for air defense. He intended to defend Britain through a strong offensive capability.

Unlike Douhet and Mitchell, Trenchard espoused his ideas not through the public or military press, but primarily through his staff, the Staff College, and RAF doctrinal publications. He was not a gifted communicator, but used his talent as an organizational leader to further his theories.[21] He remained CAS until 1929 and was closely associated with the RAF for many years, so the RAF's doctrinal publications during this time bear his influence.

Purpose of an Air Force

During World War I, Hugh Trenchard was convinced the ground force was the decisive combat arm. His intention was to support the ground army with the RAF, even after its independent status was decreed. His intended targets, railroad yards, bridges, and road networks, were more reflective of an interdiction campaign than the strategic campaign he was noted for later. This was due to his desire to coordinate air operations with the British Army.[22]

12

After World War I, the continued independence of the RAF was a major institutional concern. Trenchard used it to police Great Britain's many colonies, saving money and lives compared to estimated costs for an emphasis on ground operations. He used the mission of strategic bombing as another reason to maintain independence. The claimed decisiveness of strategic airpower and the lesser expense required to generate it in an era when Great Britain could not afford a large military was a favorite argument.[23]

Trenchard emerged from Word War I with several core beliefs. An air force's primary task was to defeat the enemy air force, as air superiority was a requirement for military success. Airpower was inherently offensive. Airpower's psychological effects outweighed its material effects. After air superiority was achieved, an air force was to destroy the morale of the enemy and damage military and naval armaments. They were to do this by targeting enemy lines of communications and munitions factories, and other centers essential for the enemy's resistance. On the subject of targeting, Trenchard was more vague than on other issues.[24]

Trenchard saw the role of the air force as the primary means to ensure the defense of Great Britain. The RAF would accomplish this through offensive air attacks on an enemy's industrial infrastructure. These attacks would shatter the enemy's civilian morale, prompting the enemy population to force its government to seek an end to the conflict.[25]

Priorities of Airpower

Immediately after World War I, Trenchard believed air superiority was the most important role for the air force. Later, his views shifted so that he believed the first priority of an air force was to defend one's country through its offensive application of airpower. As stated in AP 1300, *The Royal Air Force War Manual* in 1928, the strategic bombing campaign was the primary task. Air superiority was not a prerequisite to the strategic air campaign, which would attack objectives having the greatest potential to weaken the enemy's resistance, such as production centers, supply, communications and transportation, all military-related targets. Air superiority would be achieved by forcing the enemy to divert his air effort from the offensive to the defensive. Trenchard explicitly avoided targeting civilians to induce terror, but wanted to disrupt the livelihoods of industrial workers for the effect it would have on the enemy's morale and military readiness.[26]

Proposed Air Force Composition

The highest possible value was placed on offensive airpower. This was due partly to Trenchard's belief that offensive airpower was the stronger form of war, but also to his low confidence in the ability of interceptor aircraft to find and defeat attacking bombers. He did allow for some air defense interceptors and guns, not to effectively defeat bombers, but rather to support domestic morale. His recommended ratio was two bombers for every fighter.[27]

Impact on Germany

The *Reichswehr* devoted time and energy to the study of foreign armies and air forces, especially theorists. The primary army journal, *Militarwochenblatt*, regularly contained articles on aviation topics. Among these were articles on Air Marshal Trenchard. His speeches to British military audiences were also translated for the journal. The Germans were very interested in his views on strategic bombing. Hans Ritter, a former member of the general staff and a military commentator, discussed Trenchard's theories in his book, *The Air War,* published in 1926. Ritter's *The War of the Future and its Weapons* also covered major airpower theorists such as Trenchard.[28] Although aware of Trenchard and his theories, German theorists did not make a conscious effort to emulate him while building doctrine and force structure.

Brigadier General William M. "Billy" Mitchell

Billy Mitchell was commissioned as a second lieutenant in the Signal Corps in 1898. He spent time in the Philippines, Cuba, Alaska, and Fort Leavenworth as he gained experience and became a member of the Army General Staff in 1912. He paid for his own flight training during 1916 to 1917, after which he was sent to Europe to observe French and British air operations.

14

During this period he had the opportunity to meet with Major General Hugh Trenchard. He was subsequently appointed head of the Army Expeditionary Force's Aviation Service. He served in many command positions during the war and was appointed Assistant Chief of the Air Service after the war. He used this position to further his views on airpower and the position of the Army Air Corps in the United States.[29]

Mitchell believed the airplane fundamentally changed the defensive setting of the US. The airplane's ability to travel much farther and faster than previous means of transportation removed the isolation the US had previously counted on as part of its security.[30] He was a forceful proponent of increasing the aeronautical capabilities of the US, including both civilian and military aviation. He also felt the US was ideally suited to take advantage of aviation technology, with its moral strength, industrial capacity, and raw materials.

Purpose of an Air Force

General Mitchell had very definite views on the role of an air force within a nation's military. He felt the air force was the only truly independent service, because only aircraft could operate in the air and avoid the limitations of terrain.[31] His theories were primarily oriented toward the US and he allowed that a nation's specific situation would dictate how it would use airpower. He voiced his theories in terms of how best the US could carry out what he saw as its primary military missions.

According to Mitchell, the primary aspects of national defense were domestic tranquility, protection of coasts and frontiers, control of sea lines of communications, and the prosecution of an offensive war across the seas. He assigned the army the tasks of domestic tranquility and offensive wars on the enemy's territory. It would also gain and hold bases for air operations. Airpower would be crucial for protecting coasts and frontiers, assisting in controlling sea lines of communications and gaining air dominance in support of offensive operations. The navy would control sea lines of communications using subsurface forces. Surface forces were vulnerable and

15

no longer had utility.[32] Mitchell used his successful bombing tests against old surface ships in June and July 1921 as proof of surface ship vulnerability to aircraft.

General Mitchell advocated the use of aircraft and submarines in part because of the operating advantages they enjoyed, but also due to lower costs. He estimated that the cost of one battleship was equal to the cost of 4,000 aircraft. He also cited the significant cost of coastal defense installations. He felt Germany had proven the superiority of submarines and the vulnerabilities of surface combatants during World War I.[33]

Mitchell stressed the creation of an independent organization responsible for airpower. This organization would have coequal status with the army and navy within a proposed department of national defense. A separate service with control over its budget could be more effective in training and acquiring the right mix of personnel and equipment.[34]

Airpower was to play an important role in the national defense. Its greatest service was to be its attacks against enemy manufacturing, railroads, and shipping at great distances from friendly territory. These attacks on concentrations of enemy strength would also force the enemy air force to fight in defense of its power, providing a means to destroy the enemy's air forces.[35]

Air forces were to be in charge of air defense. The only viable defense against air attack was friendly pursuit aircraft. The air force would also command other air defense assets, such as listening and reporting posts, searchlights, cannons, and guns.[36]

Priorities of Airpower

According to Mitchell, the first mission for an air force was to attack and destroy the enemy's air forces. Air battles would play a prominent part in this destruction. After this was accomplished, the air force was to attack the enemy's tactical and strategic formations, both on the ground and the water. Both of these missions could be considered primary. The secondary mission was auxiliary support to army troops, including attacks on the enemy's fielded forces and observation.[37]

An aerial siege of the enemy's communications was part of the strategic bombing campaign. Aircraft would bomb surface communication modes and railroads and hamper the enemy's ability to use its ports. Aircraft would utilize both bombs and gas to force city evacuations, in turn destroying industrial production.[38]

Mitchell felt offensive airpower provided the key to quick and lasting results. Directly bombing the enemy's sources of power would create better overall conditions in war by shortening the conflict. This strategy would be less expensive compared with massive land armies and naval forces. Modern warfare required the support of large industries, such as steel, oil, and chemical, which are vulnerable and also irreplaceable during a short war's timeline. A short war, of course, was the objective of Mitchell's application of airpower. Concerning targeting, Mitchell wrote:

> Aircraft will attack centers of production of all kinds, means of transportation, agricultural areas, ports, and shipping, not so much the people themselves. They will destroy the means of making war.[39]

Proposed Air Force Composition

General Mitchell's views were unlike Douhet's and Trenchard's concerning force composition. His proposal for gaining control of the sky differed from Douhet's in that he placed more credence in the ability of aircraft to defend against the enemy's air force.

Pursuit aircraft, which are referred to as fighter aircraft today, were a crucial part of Mitchell's plans. To Mitchell, they were the "infantry" of the air force. Pursuit aircraft were the means to win control of the air because they were the primary means to fight and defeat the enemy's pursuit aircraft. A core competency of an air force was its ability to defeat an enemy's pursuit force. In his writings in 1921 and in *Winged Defense* in 1925, Mitchell proposed a two-to-one ratio for pursuits to bombers and attack aircraft to enable pursuit to defend friendly airspace and escort bomber and attack aircraft over enemy territory. Later, he changed to emphasize bombers much more heavily.

17

The bombardment force was the means by which the enemy's sources of strength would be attacked. Bomber aircraft would destroy objects on the ground or water with projectiles, gas, torpedoes, or even glide bombs. Mitchell envisioned the use of standoff weapons as well.

Attack aircraft would also strike surface targets, but with a different purpose. They would attack from low altitude, as low as 200 to 300 feet. Their targets would be ships, railroads, and motor transport convoys. Attack aircraft would also be used as a demoralizing force against undisciplined troops.[40]

Impact on Germany

German officers were interested in General Mitchell's ideas because of his airpower advocacy and his service against Germany in World War I. His works were well read in Germany in the 1920s. *Militarwochenblatt*, the primary journal of the German army, contained translations of Mitchell's articles, "How We Should Organize an Air Force" on 18 June 1925 and "The Era of Aviation" on 25 February 1925. The journal also covered the trials in which Mitchell's bombers sank the ex-USS *Alabama* and SMS *Ostfriesland* in 1921. In 1926, Hans Ritter discussed Mitchell's theories in *The Air War*. The Reichswehr air staff would have read of Mitchell and his ideas in American journals, including *U.S. Air Services*, to which it subscribed. German officers visited U.S. Army Air Corps installations during this time as well, bringing back what military manuals and literature they could.[41] Mitchell's efforts to develop an independent air force were most pertinent to German air officers in the interwar period.

Conclusion

Each theorist grappled with the problem of applying airpower toward the national aim of militarily defeating an enemy. They agreed that a nation had several sources of power, often referred to as centers of gravity today. They also agreed that airpower could be a decisive force in attacking these sources of power. The core source of power was the national will, demonstrated by its will to fight. The other sources of power were defined as the population, industrial capacity, and military forces. They differed on what source of power was the most important to attack to defeat national will. They also differed to varying degrees in how an air force should be constructed and utilized. Later chapters will show how German air doctrine used these elements of strategic airpower theory in its air doctrine.

2   42

---

[1]Phillip S. Meilinger, "Trenchard and 'Morale Bombing': The Evolution of Royal Air Force Doctrine Before World War II," *The Journal of Military History* 60 (April 1996): 244.

[2]Claudio G. Segre, "Douhet in Italy: Prophet Without Honor?" *Aerospace Historian* 26 (June 1979): 70-73.

[3]Giulio Douhet, *The Command of the Air,* trans. Dino Ferrari (New York: Coward-McCann, 1942; reprint, Washington, DC: Office of Air Force History, 1983), 5-6.

[4]Ibid., vii-viii.

[5]Edward Warner, "Douhet, Mitchell, Seversky: Theories of Air Warfare," in *Makers of Modern Strategy: Military Thought from Machiavelli to Hitler,* ed. Edward Mead Earle (Princeton, NJ: Princeton University Press, 1943; reprint, Princeton, NJ: Princeton University Press, 1971), 489-490.

[6]Douhet, *The Command of the Air,* 10-12.

[7]Warner, "Douhet, Mitchell, Seversky: Theories of Air Warfare," 490.

[8]David R. Mets, *The Air Campaign: John Warden and the Classic Airpower Theorists* (Maxwell Air Force Base, AL: Air University Press, 1999), 12-13.

[9]Douhet, *The Command of the Air,* 59.

[10]Frank Joseph Cappelluti, "The Life and Thoughts of Giulio Douhet" (Ph.D. diss., Rutgers University, 1967), 217-219.

[11]Warner, "Douhet, Mitchell, Seversky: Theories of Air Warfare," 490.

[12]Cappelluti, "The Life and Thoughts of Giulio Douhet," 231.

[13]OKC, Generalstab 8, Abteilung, 22.11.1944, "The Douhet Theory and Its Application to the Present War," Air Historical Branch Translation No. VII/11, USAFHRC 512.621 VII/11. This document is available at the US Air Force Historical Research Center, Maxwell AFB, AL.

[14]David Irving, *The Rise and Fall of the Luftwaffe: The Life of Field Marshal Erhard Milch* (Boston: Little, Brown and Company, 1973), 27.

[15]Richard Suchenwirth, *The Development of the German Air Force, 1919-1939* (New York: Arno Press, 1970), 93.

[16]Werner Baumbach, *The Life and Death of the Luftwaffe* (New York: Ballantine Books, 1949), 7.

[17]Adolf Galland, "Defeat of the Luftwaffe: Fundamental Causes," *Air University Quarterly Review* 6, no.1 (spring 1953): 23.

[18]Phillip S. Meilinger, "Trenchard and 'Morale Bombing': The Evolution of Royal Air Force Doctrine Before World War II," 247.

[19]Ibid., 243-244.

[20]Mets, *The Air Campaign: John Warden and the Classic Airpower Theorists*, 22.

[21]Meilinger, "Trenchard and 'Morale Bombing': The Evolution of Royal Air Force Doctrine Before World War II," 256-257.

[22]Ibid., 249.

[23]Ibid., 253-255.

[24]Ibid., 255-256.

[25]Mets, *The Air Campaign: John Warden and the Classic Airpower Theorists*, 26.

[26]Meilinger, "Trenchard and 'Morale Bombing': The Evolution of Royal Air Force Doctrine Before World War II," 258-260.

[27]Ibid., 255-256.

[28]James S. Corum, *The Luftwaffe: Creating the Operational Air War, 1918-1940* (Lawrence, KS: The University Press of Kansas, 1997), 69-70.

[29]Mark A. Clodfelter, "Molding Airpower Convictions: Development and Legacy of William Mitchell's Strategic Thought," in *The Paths of Heaven: The Evolution of Airpower Theory,* ed. Phillip S. Meilinger (Maxwell Air Force Base, AL: Air University Press, 1997), 79-91.

[30]William Mitchell, *Winged Defense: The Development and Possibilities of Modern Air Power, Economic and Military* (New York: G. P. Putnam's Sons, 1925), xi.

[31]Ibid., xv.

[32]Ibid., 101-102, 109.

[33]Ibid., 102-110.

[34]Ibid., xix.

[35]Ibid., 188-190.

[36]Ibid., 203.

[37]Robert Frank Futrell, *Ideas, Concepts, Doctrine: Basic Thinking in the United States Air Force 1907-1960* (Maxwell Air Force Base, AL: Air University Press, 1989), 33-34.

[38]Mitchell, *Winged Defense*, 5.

[39]Ibid., 16-17.

[40]Ibid., 164-171, 183-190.

[41]Corum, *The Luftwaffe: Creating the Operational Air War, 1918-1940*, 69-70, 301.

[42]

CHAPTER 3

LESSONS FROM WORLD WAR I

Giulio Douhet, Hugh Trenchard, and Billy Mitchell were indeed prominent airpower

theorists and to a varying degree prolific writers and speakers on behalf of airpower,

predominantly the use of airpower in an independent, strategic role. They gained experience

serving in leadership positions during World War I, from which they developed many of their

ideas. German officers discussed and read their theories and used them as references when

deliberating the role airpower would play in a future German air force. However, foreign

experience in the recent conflict was not the only relevant data point. Germany had its own

experience from World War I to influence its decision makers. Ground and air warfare lessons

were germane in influencing the role airpower would play in pre-World War II German military

doctrine.

German Experience

Strategic Air Warfare

The Luftstreitkrafte, the German Army Air Service, implemented the first strategic air

offensive during World War I, initially using *Zeppelin* airships and later fixed-wing bombers. It

was designed to attack the morale of the British people while the submarine force attacked the

war economy. The air and submarine efforts were parallel efforts to knock Great Britain from the

war.[1] The failure of the army campaigns in 1916 and the ensuing stalemate of 1917 promoted a

greater interest in strategic bombing than earlier in the war. Improvements in technology,

aircraft, bombs, sights, and training made long-range bombardment appear more viable. Distant

targets became legitimate objectives[2]

Originally, the German Navy conducted raids on the British Isles using *Zeppelins*, but

these were halted due to the vulnerability of huge, hydrogen-filled airships. Later, in 1917, the

German air service fielded *Gotha* IV bombers that could reach Great Britain with 1,000 pounds of bombs, and the *Riesen Gigant* that could deliver a 3,900-pound payload. With these aircraft General Eric Ludendorff supported the resumption of a strategic bombing campaign to create a morale crisis and convince Great Britain to end the conflict.[3]

Summary of German Strategic Offensive

Zeppelin attacks on Great Britain were initiated in 1915 primarily to create panic in order to cause the British to discontinue participation in the war. From 1915 to 1916, 220 Zeppelin sorties were flown against Great Britain. They dropped 175 tons of bombs, killing 557 Britons and causing damage valued at 1.5 million pounds. Nine Zeppelins were lost during these raids.[4]

From 25 May 1917 to 20 May 1918, German fixed-wing *Gotha* and *Riesenflugzeug*, or *Gigant*, bombers conducted twenty-seven raids on Great Britain, seventeen of which were made on London. Once again, the intention was to make war on the morale of the British people. Industry, communications, supply dumps, and cross channel traffic were the intended targets. Two of the most notable raids were on 13 June 1917, which caused 162 killed and 432 injured and on 7 July 1917, with 54 killed and 190 injured. These raids graphically demonstrated the vulnerability of Great Britain to air attack and influenced the British leaders to firm-up home defense. Overall, these raids caused 835 deaths and 1,935 injured British civilians, and damage valued at over 1,400,000 pounds. Sixty-two bombers were lost during these 413 sorties.[5] British losses may not have been significant compared to battlefield casualties, but their occurrence in an area previously thought isolated from continental warfare was significant to future British policy and thought.

Perceived Results

The Germans concluded that the results of the *Gotha* and *Riesen* raids were not in proportion to the effort expended, similar to their conclusion regarding the Zeppelin raids of 1915 and 1916. German analysts concluded after the war that they were causing twenty-three casualties per ton of bombs dropped on England. They did not see sufficient material or moral damage inflicted on the British to justify continued raids.[6]

The Germans also concluded that a strategic air campaign was not a quick strategy to win a war. It started a precedent that the other side could honor by conducting a retaliatory air campaign. It also diverted essential resources from the field armies. The last reason was perhaps more important, because the army's field generals felt the most important function of aviation was the protection of fielded forces.[7] These forces were the decisive combat arms during World War I.

A German analysis of the RAF bombing effort against Germany showed a low regard for its effectiveness. Thirty-one raids were conducted against German towns in July 1918, but ten of these produced no casualties and little damage. Most casualties from bombing raids were avoidable. The first time a city was bombed, people wanted to observe the attacks. On subsequent raids, people took cover, and casualties dropped.[8] Air raid sirens that disrupted the work routines of industrial workers caused most of the problems from British bombing. German analysts noted that although civilians feared bombing, there was slight material damage.[9]

Costs of the Offensive

The German Air Service lost sixty-two bombers during its strategic air campaigns of 1917 and 1918. Of these, thirty-eight *Gotha* and *Riesen* bombers were lost due to operational accidents. German air leadership had learned the British air defenses were more effective during daylight, and so conducted nineteen attacks at night. They considered the campaign a failure because of the high cost in aircrews and aircraft, mainly due to problems with aircraft and pilots, and adapting them to the night flying environment. These operational factors were as significant as the air defenses in the perceived failure of the campaign.[10]

Air Defense

24

The Luftstreitkrafte was an effective air defense organization during World War I. It shot down opponents at better than a two-to-one ratio. These efforts were oriented to homeland defense as well as to the battlefield. The 1918 Allied strategic bombing campaign suffered greatly due to the defensive efforts of the German air defenders, losing 352 British aircraft and 264 aircrew dead or missing, or one aircraft for every 1.54 tons of bombs dropped. The British loss in aircraft and equipment was more monetarily damaging to Great Britain than the damage they inflicted on Germany.[11] Germany had developed effective air defense and civil defense systems, so the effects of the British bombing efforts were minimized. Germany did suffer 797 dead, 380 wounded, and 15 million marks in damage, enough to see the bombing campaign as a threat, but one that could be defended against with some success.[12] Germany learned that air defenses were effective enough to stymie a strategic air campaign.

Other Lessons

The Germans also learned the value of interdiction. After the war Captain Hans Ritter wrote of the possibility of crippling an army by shutting off its supply routes. He specifically referred to the Battle of Verdun, where the Germans were unable to destroy the French major supply route. He felt that had Germany successfully interdicted this road, it would have won at Verdun.

The inaccuracy of contemporary bombing was also demonstrated. The German Air Service had attempted to strike the Woolwich arsenal near London for over three years. It was only able to obtain one solid hit during that campaign.[13]

The German Air Service operated as a defensive force on the battlefield. Although highly successful in air-to-air fighting, it did so primarily over its own side of the battlefield. The Allied air forces gained the initiative by fighting the war on the German side of the lines, which cost them more crews and planes, but brought them air superiority. Germany learned airpower was offensive and an air force should seek out and destroy the enemy air forces.[14]

25

Ground Warfare

The German General Staff traditionally stressed mobility in its operational plans. It wanted to use flank attacks, envelopments, and encirclement battles of attrition. It would exploit its advantages of interior lines of communications. Railroad technology would be used in pursuit of mobilization. The Germans hoped to exploit the speed of its mobilization and concentration to dictate the time and place of battle to the enemy. The Staff was cognizant that Germany had enemies on several fronts and needed to use speed to dictate where and when it would face its enemies, so that it could face them sequentially.[15] World War I would pose some problems to the German plans and provide the German military an opportunity to reevaluate them after the war.

Western Front

Germany encountered major problems attempting to accomplish its operational objectives. In 1914, the German Army failed to interfere significantly with French mobilization. It was unsuccessful in preventing the redeployment of the French reserves. German foot soldiers and horses lacked the necessary stamina for encirclement operations over great distances. General Hans von Seeckt, the first Chief of the *Truppenamt* in 1919, the postwar clandestine General Staff, and Army Commander from 1920 to 1926, viewed motorized transport as a solution to some of these problems. In 1921, the German Army conducted exercises with motorized infantry, motor transport, and tanks to achieve greater mobility.[16]

The German Army also learned that tactics were an answer to the problem of assaulting prepared defensive positions equipped with modern firepower. *"Hutier"* infiltration tactics were used on the eastern front, Caporetto, and in Ludendorff's offensives on the Western Front in 1918. Short artillery bombardments and specially trained infantry "stormtroopers" were key elements of the German tactics. Cooperation and teamwork among all combat arms was essential. Insufficient mobility was still a problem, since stormtroopers could not be reinforced or resupplied quickly.[17] The air service had created a ground support doctrine in 1917, and was one of the combat arms expected to team with the infantry. The Halberstadt CLII and CLIV and Hannoveraner aircraft were examples of aircraft specialized for ground attack. Ground attack squadrons performed live-fire training with infantry units to prepare for the 1918 offensive.[18]

One technological advance the Germans did not make full use of was the tank. The German Army did use tracked vehicles and did have access to captured Allied tanks. Engineers were able to modify Allied designs and develop their own versions. However, the tank was given a relatively low priority by the high command. General Ludendorff was also not impressed by the tank. Many German army officers felt the tank played an important part in the Allied victory, after seeing its performance at Cambrai, Amiens, and Soissons. Ludendorff and the high command felt that the solution to static warfare was mobility more than firepower.[19]

Eastern Front

The eastern front battles adhered to traditional German theories on ground warfare. Infantry and artillery cooperation, stormtroop tactics, surprise, and mobility were factors in the east while the west was characterized by static operations. Many successful offensives occurred in Poland, Italy, Romania, and Russia. The German Army witnessed maneuver warfare in the east over open terrain. In the spring of 1915, the Eleventh Army moved 6.5 miles a day over a period of six weeks during the Gorlice offensive against Russia. Independent motorized operations were conducted in Romania in November 1916. Many German leaders of 1935 to 1945, including Rommel, Kesselring, and von Manstein, served on the Eastern Front. Development of squad tactics emphasizing infiltration, rapid advance, and bypass of strongpoints was facilitated by the conditions of the eastern front. The successful German and Austrian armies used stormtroop tactics against the Italian army at Caporetto in October and November 1917.[20]

German Lessons

27

The post-World War I German military system was built upon the foundations of military defeat. The German General Staff concluded after the war that by its very nature, Germany would lose several types of wars. A long war would be extremely tough to win, because it would threaten trade for an extended period of time. A coalition of enemies and a multifront war would also spell certain defeat. Germany had to fight a fast offensive war so that it could avoid a multifront war and prevent coalitions from building combat power. Aviation would best serve German military needs by supporting a fast war to prevent a war of exhaustion or a stalemate.[21]

Based on its geography and weakened condition after the war, Germany continued to need a capable land army to repel invaders. Airpower could not be considered a substitute for a strong and effective army. From its experience, it retained a belief in the superiority of flexible and mobile tactics in the defense and the offense. It also believed in the superiority of its training and its air strategy. Its primary problem was solving the superiority of allied technology in certain areas, such as armored vehicles. Overall, the fundamental aim of German military tactics remained annihilation using the preferred maneuvers of double and single envelopment.[22]

British Experience

Strategic Air Warfare

Major General Trenchard accepted command of the Independent Air Force in France in July 1918. His task was to carry out the strategic air campaign envisioned by British leadership since the *Gotha* raids on London the previous year. In July 1918, the British forces conducted thirty-one bombing raids that killed thirty-three civilians. From July to November 1918, the RAF dropped 543 tons of bombs and lost 352 aircraft. The bomber forces suffered 29 aircrew killed, 64 wounded, and 235 missing. They lost 1.54 aircraft for every ton of bombs dropped.[23]

Results of the German Offensive

The British saw immediate effects, predominately moral, from the German raids in 1917, especially those on 13 June and 7 July. Panic in London caused widespread clamor for increased homeland defense. As a result, three fighter squadrons were withdrawn from the battlefield in France for rear defense. Rising absenteeism and falling productivity in industrial plants due to the bombing raids greatly concerned the War Cabinet.[24]

While the Germans felt the bombing raids were not sufficiently effective, the British drew different lesson from the *Gotha* raids. These operations forced the British to reevaluate their use of airpower. Following a study of British airpower by the Smuts committee, the Royal Air Force and the Air Ministry were formed. These organizations would be the means for Britain's own strategic air offensive, intended to hit the chief industrial centers of Germany.

The British intended to respond to the Germans with their own independent bombing campaign. This campaign drew support at several levels, including Prime Minister Lloyd George, Parliament, and the public. This support was critical to a strategic campaign, as the French had earlier discovered. The goal was continuous, intense pressure on Germany, not simply a reprisal.

CAS General Frederick Sykes stated the position of the RAF in his memo of 27 June 1918. He felt a long-range bombardment offensive was the most important function of military aviation. Bombers should be employed to attack two similar target systems. First were the specific target systems of munitions, submarine construction, chemicals, steel, machine engineering, and magnetos. Second were densely populated industrial centers to destroy the morale of the workers. The Ruhr region possessed many such targets.[25]

The British predicted that strategic bombing attacks would produce widespread terror. This may have been due to the RAF leadership's interpretation of the results of the German raids. The Germans had dropped 300 tons of bombs, causing 4,820 casualties and 1,413 dead. They did cause panic in London and a diversion of fighters from France to Great Britain for homeland defense.

Results of the British Offensive

The actual results of the air offensive against Germany disappointed investigators after the war. The attacks on railroad stations and rail junctions were ineffective. The British did see value to their attacks on the Rhineland, even if the material damage was not significant. The raids succeeded in keeping workers awake at night, which caused lower productivity. Air raid sirens sounded more often than actual raids, and in some cities, over ten times as often. British analysts placed much more credence in the moral and harassing effect of their bombing than the Germans did.[26] The Germans saw the same evidence, but recognized little effect because the material damage was relatively minor. The British rationalization of the material ineffectiveness was counterbalanced by Trenchard's claim that morale effects were twenty times greater than material effects.[27]

One lesson that the British learned as well as the Germans was the cost of conducting a strategic air campaign. An air campaign appeared to have a low cost initially, because it offered the lure of avoiding sizable armies. This turned out to be false because of the depth of industry required to equip the required number of bomber squadrons, train the crews, and supply the units. The Germans halted their offensive in part because of the cost of building the aircraft themselves. The British could better absorb the large costs of building such an air force.

The RAF relied on their wartime experience when conducting a study in 1923 on the possible effects of a strategic offensive by the French Air Force. The study concluded that by 1925 the French could drop 100 tons per day, with each ton producing fifty casualties, one-third of which would be deaths. In comparison, the Germans dropped 150 tons per day in 1940, each ton producing seven casualties.[28] Thus, experience caused the British to place great credence in

30

the ability of an air force equipped with current technology to launch a decisive strategic air campaign and for such a campaign to cause great casualties.

Ground Warfare Lessons

British leadership felt the general carnage of war among industrial powers was a disaster. Even during the war the human cost seriously troubled the senior political and military leadership. The war cost Britain 750,000 dead, nine percent of its men under age forty-five. British wounded numbered 1,500,000. The costs weighed heavily on the British leadership, who consequently placed a high priority on avoiding a repeat of a continental war.[29]

Western Front

British, as well as French and American, tactical experience was primarily on the western front. The environment was a static battlefield consisting of a long line of trenches from 1915 through 1917. The British solution to the static front, caused by the massive firepower available to the armies, was to mount firepower on armored vehicles. The tank, although experiencing problems initially, proved to be a significant factor in later battles.[30]

Although it was one of the victors, Great Britain did not desire to remain a continental land power. A large army would be more likely to be involved in another ground war of attrition, whose cost it wanted to avoid. Remaining apart from continental alliances would help to avoid another ground war. Britain associated a high cost with a ground war, not with an air war.

British Lessons

Britain's experience reinforced her desire for a traditional British campaign using sea power, commercial and economic strength, and allies. Prime Minister Neville Chamberlain felt it was best to employ her resources in air and naval campaigns. Bombing became synonymous with a rapid decisive air offensive of great destructiveness. General war became synonymous with a long attrition campaign of great destruction. Both engendered fear among British politicians and leaders. The result was a reluctance to enter into war. The RAF's strategic air force was to be

31

used in a deterrence role, in combination with the blockade strategy. If war was necessary, it was to be fought at a minimal cost to Great Britain, and so airpower became the preferable way to attack an enemy, thus avoiding the use of ground combat. British strategists had a very real fear of a "knock-out blow" air strike, and wanted to deter that possible bombing attack with a threat of their own.[31]

Conclusion

Although Germany lost the war, it did not look for airpower to revolutionize its approach to military doctrine. Instead, it looked for airpower and technology to improve the way it fought its traditional doctrine. The German lessons from World War I tended to reinforce their belief in the utility of the offensive in modern warfare. They were fully aware of their need to be engaged on the European continent and their inability to escape a continental land war. They saw lessons from the war in terms of how they could be applied in pursuit of a quick victory on the ground. Air warfare lessons were heeded, but were seen in the larger context of a continental war and in support of a victory on the ground. Contemporary theorists were studied, but Germany drew more on its own experience in modern warfare and its environment after the war. These lessons suggested that airpower would be a major part of Germany's desire to fight and win short wars. Airpower would be an element of a combined arms team.

British lessons reinforced their traditional efforts to avoid land warfare on the continent and, and implied a dramatic shift in its security environment. The Royal Navy no longer provided the only defense for the home islands. Airpower was the means by which Great Britain would be threatened, as well as the means by which it could avoid extended ground combat. Hugh Trenchard was the spokesman for some of the British lessons, and one of many who influenced British doctrine. Great Britain was a victor, but resolved to avoid participation in such land wars in the future. It wanted to use airpower similarly to the way it had traditionally used its maritime and economic strengths to avoid extended continental conflicts. These lessons pointed to the future adoption of airpower as a strategic asset and the adoption of strategic air campaigns independent from land campaigns as an element of military strategy.

---

[1]James S. Corum, "The Development of Strategic Air War Concepts in Interwar Germany, 1919-1939," *Air Power History* 44, no. 4 (winter 1997): 21.

[2]Richard J. Overy, "Strategic Bombardment before 1939: Doctrine, Planning, and Operations," in *Case Studies in Strategic Bombardment,* ed. R. Cargill Hall (Washington, DC: U.S. Government Printing Office, 1998), 15.

[3]Ibid., 17.

[4]David Divine, *The Broken Wing: A Study in the British Exercise of Air Power* (London: Hutchinson and Co., 1966), 102; Raymond H. Fredette, *The Sky on Fire: The First Battle of Britain, 1917-1918, and the Birth of the Royal Air Force* (New York: Harcourt Brace Jovanovich, 1976; reprint, Washington, DC: Smithsonian Institution Press, 1991), 262-266; and Overy, 14.

[5]Lee Kennett, *A History of Strategic Bombing* (New York: Charles Scribner's Sons, 1982), 23-25; Divine, 102-105; and Fredette, 262-266.

[6]Fredette, 196, 237.

[7]Overy, 17.

[8]Corum, "The Development of Strategic Air War Concepts," 21-22.

[9]Overy, 24.

[10]Divine, 110; Fredette, 266; and Kennett, 45.

[11]James S. Corum, "The Old Eagle as Phoenix: The Luftstreitkrafte Creates an Operational Air War Doctrine, 1919-1920," *Air Power History* 39, no. 1 (spring 1997): 14.

[12]Ibid., 14.

[13]Kennett, 48-49.

[14]James S. Corum, "Airpower Thought in Continental Europe between the Wars," in *The Paths of Heaven: The Evolution of Airpower Theory,* ed. Phillip S. Meilinger (Maxwell Air Force Base, AL: Air University Press, 1997), 169-170.

[15]Barry R. Posen, *The Sources of Military Doctrine* (Ithaca, NY: Cornell University Press, 1984), 183.

[16]Ibid., 190.

[17]Ibid., 190.

[18]Corum, "The Old Eagle as Phoenix," 14; and James S. Corum, *The Roots of Blitzkrieg: Hans von Seeckt and German Military Reform* (Lawrence, KS: The University Press of Kansas, 1992), 7-9, 15.

[19]Corum, *The Roots of Blitzkrieg, 20-23.*

[20]Ibid., 7-9.

[21]Hauptmann Hermann, *The Luftwaffe: Its Rise and Fall* (New York: G. P. Putnam's Sons, 1943), 142-143.

[22]Overy, 28; Corum, *The Roots of Blitzkrieg*, 24; and Posen, 190.

[23]Corum, *The Roots of Blitzkrieg,*17-18.

[24]Kennett, 26.

[25]Overy, 17-18.

[26]Kennett, 51.

[27]Overy, 26.

[28]Posen, 145.

[29]Ibid., 144.

[30]Corum, *The Roots of Blitzkrieg,*7; and Posen, 191.

[31]Posen, 145-146.

1

CHAPTER 4

POST-WORLD WAR I ENVIRONMENT

Several factors shaped the national security environments of both Germany and Great

Britain after World War I. The Treaty of Versailles affected the means by which Germany could

arm herself militarily. Its relationships with its neighbors helped to decide potential enemies.

After Adolf Hitler assumed Germany's political leadership, his political goals also fashioned

Germany's military goals. Great Britain, meanwhile, had colonial interests outside Europe, as

well as interests in Europe. Resources constrained the ability of both countries to develop

military means to aid their political goals. The strategic environment and the constraints affecting

the two nations were influential in determining how strategic airpower would be pursued and

implemented by each. The post-World War I environment propelled Britain toward a strategic

bomber doctrine and Germany toward an all-purpose air doctrine.

Tradition

Germany

The German military traditionally believed the decisive battles of a war occurred at the

outset, making for short wars.[2] German military leadership was concerned that a long war would

limit the military's dominance over the planning and control of a war. Long wars would also

increase the importance of social and economic factors in the outcome of the war. A long war

would require economic mobilization, which in turn would require a shift in resources from the

military to food and raw material storage, and a shift of people from the ranks of the military to

the ranks of skilled laborers. Preparation for a long war and the underlying industrial and

logistical bases would reduce the military strength needed to win a short war. So, preparation for

a long war, a war of attrition, would create the conditions for a long war. Instead, Germany relied

upon a shock strategy with which to win a war of annihilation, typified by the Schlieffen Plan implemented in 1914. Although Germany did have some voices warning of long wars, such as von Moltke in 1890 and Max Warburg in 1907, the dominant theme was in favor of a short war.[3]

The military lessons from World War I reinforced Germany's belief in the offensive to prosecute a short war of annihilation and that the decisive battle would take place at the beginning of a war.[4] Germany's continental position made it vulnerable to a blockade and disruption of its overseas lines of communication and was a major reason behind the favored short war. Its leaders were keenly aware of its limited natural resources and its greater vulnerability to loss of those resources than its potential enemies. By its geographical position, Germany could not easily avoid a land engagement on the European continent should war come, and its land warfare dominance continued. Prior to World War I, land warfare had dominated naval warfare in German military thinking; after the war, it dominated air warfare.

After World War I, the *Reichswehr*, Germany's military force, returned to its strategic roots. The German General Staff stressed mobility to facilitate flank attacks, envelopments, and encirclement battles of annihilation. The tradition of exploiting interior lines of communication and railroad technology were also present in order to use its speed of mobilization and concentration to dictate the time and place of battle to the enemy. With enemies on several fronts, the staff desired to face them sequentially. The *Reichswehr* favored its traditional offensive doctrine to fight its enemies, and desired to adapt new technology to its traditional doctrines.[5]

Great Britain

Great Britain was traditionally a maritime colonial power. British lessons reinforced their traditional efforts to avoid land warfare on the continent and the increased potential threats to the home islands. It had traditionally used its maritime and economic power to avoid extended continental conflicts. It also had a long history of participating in coalition warfare, although not as a member of extensive peacetime alliances. The exception to this policy was prior to World

War I, when Great Britain's participation in the Triple Entente was a factor in its participation in a continental land war.

As far as home defense, Great Britain had traditionally felt safe. The English Channel and the Royal Navy had proven to be two formidable obstacles to potential invaders. Now, however, the home islands were no longer isolated behind the defense of the Royal Navy. British leadership, especially the RAF leadership, viewed airpower as the means by which Great Britain would be threatened, as well as the means by which it could avoid extended ground combat. These lessons pointed to the future adoption of airpower as a strategic asset and the adoption of strategic air campaigns independent from land campaigns as an element of military strategy. Great Britain wanted to use the RAF and the new technology of air warfare to generate a new doctrine of deterrence to preserve its empire and avoid continental land warfare.

Strategic Setting

The strategic settings of Germany and Great Britain shaped each state's national interests and the military strategy adopted to support its interests.

Germany

Germany was a continental power that would face a high probability of land operations from the outset. Germany's strategic position would be damaged by enemy ground forces if it mounted strategic bombing campaigns at the national power centers of Britain, Poland, or France while its armies were losing terrain and resources in Silesia, East Prussia, and the Rhineland. Meanwhile, a preventive war was a real possibility to Hitler and Germany's military leaders as Germany rearmed.[6]

Relative Weakness

The Treaty of Versailles was signed on 28 June 1919 and had immediate effects on Germany's security environment. It removed territory and population from Germany in both the east and the west. Poland was a new neighbor to the east, as well as Czechoslovakia. The treaty

denied Germany the right to fortify its frontier and left it with a 100,000-man army, a small navy

and no air force. The treaty limited Germany to 140 aircraft and 169 engines for commercial use

only. On 9 April 1920 General von Seeckt disbanded Germany's remaining air units at the

request of the Ambassador's conference in Paris. He did not abandon hope for future air forces,

though.[7] Germany's military was relatively weaker than its neighbors, any of which could be an

adversary in a future war.

In the interwar period, Germany had identified several potential enemies, including

France, Belgium, Poland, and Czechoslovakia. France was a former wartime enemy, and played

a part in ensuring that the Versailles Treaty limited German power. France also had treaties with

Belgium, Poland, Czechoslovakia, Romania, and Yugoslavia. Much of Poland's territory was

former German territory. This was one reason Germany considered Poland an inevitable enemy.

Geographically, these countries presented a possible two front war. German military leaders

eventually considered Russia as a possible enemy as well. Hitler had initially hoped to keep

Great Britain as an ally. He looked up to the British as a great world power and hoped to have an

alliance with the British, even holding back on naval rearmament to avoid provoking Britain. It

was not until 1938 that Hitler acknowledged Great Britain as a possible enemy.[8] The only ally

Germany had in the 1930s was Italy.

An air fleet offered a possible solution to this strategic situation. It could fight an

operational level war against enemies on one or both fronts. Large numbers of two-engine

bombers and dive bombers could fight an independent battle against an enemy's war potential

and give support to the army and navy.[9] However, German military leaders did not see air forces

as a replacement for a sufficiently armed and manned army to fight and win ground battles

against the imminent threat, an enemy's army.

Desire for a Quick Victory

38

The prospect of a two-front war against a coalition with a weakened military reinforced Germany's desire to fight and defeat its enemies serially. This objective led to a desire for quick battlefield victories, which would allow the German military to complete operations before other European powers could intervene. The most important objective was to avoid a repetition of World War I's multifront, attrition warfare. This objective was in line with traditional German military thought.

Blitzkrieg was adopted because it supported speed. It focused on the enemy's command and control functions. Elements of blitzkrieg included a breakthrough of the frontline to attack the enemy's rear as quickly as possible. Mechanized formations would use speed to disrupt the enemy's movement of people, information, and machines in the rear. Airpower would destroy transportation and command nodes to produce confusion and the collapse of the enemy's combat organization. Blitzkrieg emphasized combined arms operations, and airpower was used to provide mobile firepower to effect victory on the battlefield.[10]

When Germany rearmed after 1935, Hitler desired a maximum number of aircraft and frontlines units. These numbers would provide more combat power to win a short war. The build-up of infrastructure and reserves to support a more durable force for a longer war was less important.[11] Aircraft to support blitzkrieg requirements and air superiority had to be plentiful, but did not have to feature extended range or payload. These requirements favored single- and twin-engine fighter, bomber, and reconnaissance aircraft and not large, long-range bombers.

Deterrence

After Hitler and the Nazi Party gained power in January 1933, they reorganized the air forces under the Reich Air Ministry (RLM) led by Hermann Goering. The Air Ministry's first comprehensive aircraft procurement program was the Rhineland Program in June 1934 and reflected the use of the air force as a deterrent to potential enemies. It strove to buy 3,715 aircraft during fiscal years 1934 and 1935. The preponderance of bombers compared to fighters, 822 to

39

245, indicated the higher value placed on the offensive use of airpower.[12] These bombers were not four-engine bombers, but were capable of striking centers of power in the potential enemies of Poland, France, and Czechoslovakia.

Dr. Robert Knauss, an associate of Secretary of State for Aviation General Erhard Milch when he was at Lufthansa, authored a secret memo in May 1933 urging the creation of a large heavy bomber fleet to shield Germany's rearmament. The memo had a Douhetian tone, proposing that airpower was a strategically decisive weapon. It also stated that Germany would have a two-front war if it did not rearm. The strategic situation at the time showed that Poland and France were threats to German rearmament and that a two-front war was possible. Knauss, similar to General Mitchell in the United States, argued that Germany could build 400 four-engine bombers for the same price as two battleships or five divisions. Such a bomber force would have political, diplomatic, and psychological impact and would increase the risk of war to the potential enemy should that state intervene to stop Germany's rearmament.

Hitler accepted the idea of using the Luftwaffe as a "Risk" Air Force, or *Risiko-Luftwaffe*. As a risk air force, the Luftwaffe would protect the growth of Germany's war potential by threatening potential attackers with an indiscriminate strategic air offensive against their industry and population. The political leadership imposed a strategic capability on the air force to deter potential enemies. However, this strategic capability was in the eye of the beholder, as the Germans wanted. The Luftwaffe actually had the means to be a tactical, not strategic air force.[13]

Coercion

Adolf Hitler and the Nazi Party relied upon military power as their dominant element of national power, much more so than political and economic power. When Hitler did use diplomatic means to attain his political objectives, he supported those means with the adversary's perception of Germany's military power. He used the military, especially the Luftwaffe, in a coercive manner, intending to overwhelm the opposition with a belligerent display of power.

Hitler's obsession with the image of power required fielding ready weapons over a more time consuming increase of Germany's industrial and military capacity. There was an emphasis on visible military power over industrial capacity. The image of armed might was more important than true military capability.[14]

This desire for visible power affected air rearmament. Numbers of bombers became more important than the types and capabilities of those bombers. Four-engine bombers, with their added range and payload, were more complex and resource-intensive than twin-engine bombers. Goering was very interested that industry could make 2½ twin-engine bombers for every four-engine bomber. As Goering remarked, "The Fuhrer does not ask me how big my bombers are, but how many there are."[15]

Hitler needed an immediate appearance of strength with which to pursue his political goals. A recognized weapon, bomber aircraft formations, would help inspire respect from abroad. Hitler intended to use the Luftwaffe as a means of terror to support his political objectives. Increased publicity showed the emerging air capability's strength. German officials showed foreign dignitaries their aircraft and production capabilities in order to portray a very strong Luftwaffe. Hitler used the military and this image of armed strength successfully to back up his efforts at diplomacy. Austria in February and March 1938, Sudetenland in May 1938, and Czechoslovakia in August and September 1938 were all examples of German political victories facilitated by the perceived might of Germany's air force.[16] Four-engine bombers with their longer range and payload were not necessary to intimidate Germany's neighbors.

Rise of Military Strength

The transition of Germany's air force from obscurity to perceived superiority to its neighbors required much work even before Hitler publicly announced the Luftwaffe's existence. The Treaty of Versailles severely restricted aviation activity in Germany. The only military

41

aircraft allowed were 100 seaplanes to the German Navy to search for mines. Article 201 prohibited the manufacture and import of aircraft and aircraft engines until 14 April 1922. On 5 May 1922 the Inter-Allied Aviation Inspection Committee allowed the design and manufacture of civil aircraft with the low performance figures of less than 110 knots, 170 nautical miles of range, 2.5 hours of endurance and 16,000 feet ceiling.[17] The Paris Air Agreement on 21 May 1926 removed the restrictions on civil aviation within Germany. At this time, the agreement also legalized the training of a limited number of *Reichswehr* officers in sport flying.[18]

The *Reichswehr* did not wait for the concurrence of the international community to begin rebuilding its aviation capabilities. The Treaty of Rapallo on 26 April 1922 between Germany and the Soviet Union enabled the Germans to train personnel and test equipment. Germany used an air base at Lipezk in the Soviet Union to train aircrew and test its aircraft and equipment, including bombs and aiming equipment. The aviation industry also used this opportunity to begin retooling its design and manufacturing abilities. Junkers operated an airframe and engine plant at Fili inside the USSR from 1924 to 1927. The *Reichswehr* secretly trained 450 pilots at Lipezk from 1925 to 1932 and tested one of its early bombers, the Do 11. It also conducted dive-bombing tests at Lipezk, learning the precision available from this delivery method. The future Luftwaffe gained an increase in aviation awareness among contemporary military officers, and a trained top echelon of officers.[19]

During the late 1920s and early 1930s, the *Reichswehr* researched the issue of building up an air capability. During this time, the German aircraft industry possessed a technical competence comparable to other European powers. German civilian transports flew more miles and passengers than the British, French and Italians combined. Lieutenant Colonel Hellmuth Felmy developed a study to support the mobilization of a 21-division army. The Air Force was to comprise 80 squadrons, 42 of which were to be bombers, for a 1,000 aircraft force. The high number of bombers was to knock out the enemy air force and air bases. However, a study released by the Air Inspectorate Office of the *Truppenamt* in April 1932 revealed that only

Junkers and Heinkel could perform aircraft series production.[20]

On 15 May 1933 Hermann Goering assumed control of military aviation as the Reich

Commissioner of Aviation and the Reich Air Minister. He assumed control over Secretary of

State for Air Erhard Milch on 1 September 1933. The military had only five bomber squadrons

on 1 April 1934. The RLM was to increase requirements for bombers over the next several years,

expecting to have 150 Do 11 bombers, 222 Do 13 and Do 23 bombers in addition to 450 auxiliary

bombers, such as the Ju 52 on 30 September 1935. Although obsolete, these aircraft were to

teach industry how to mass-produce aircraft. On 26 February 1935 Adolf Hitler publicly declared

the ReichsLuftwaffe an independent branch of the armed forces within the Wehrmacht to be

effective on 1 March 1935.[21]

General Felmy developed the Concentrated Aircraft Procurement Program on 7

November 1938, which was approved by Colonel Hans Jeschonnek, the Chief of the Operation

Staff. It was designed to prepare the Luftwaffe for a strategic air war against Great Britain by

1942 and called for 58 *Kampfgeschwader*, 30 of which were to be strategic, including as many

four-engine He 177 wings as possible.[22] This relatively late push for a force structure of four-

engine bombers reflects the late designation of Great Britain as a potential enemy, as well as

resource factors.

Great Britain

After World War I, Great Britain operated under the notion that another major war would

destroy its empire. Consequently, its priorities were the preservation of its empire and supporting

its European interests. Its economic and military resources were insufficient to directly

accomplish its interests with military means. Great Britain instead relied upon its traditional threat of a war of attrition using its industrial mobilization and a naval blockade. The military would concentrate on defensive naval and air forces to protect its homeland and industry and its sea lines. Behind this protection, Britain would mobilize its economic resources and seek allies when the strategic situation necessitated. These allies would be needed to fight continental land wars, a lesson Great Britain learned from World War I.[23]

Great Britain chose a deterrence strategy to preserve its interests. There were numerous British interests throughout the world. These included its colonies and the European balance of power. It perceived specific threats to those interests from Germany in Europe, Italy in the Mediterranean and Africa, and Japan in the Far East. Great Britain also had insufficient military power to confront each threat. Its adopted strategy was an offensive capability to deny its enemies the probability for immediate success and a long-term threat of ultimate imperial mobilization and a naval blockade. Prime Minister Neville Chamberlain felt that deterring Germany would be sufficient, because Japan would only attack if Britain were already at war.[24] Meanwhile, Britain's deterrence capabilities were minimal, taking the form of the RAF's bombing capability.[25]

Concerning Europe, Britain was interested in maintaining the balance of power, but had not signed any commitments. It believed its defensive frontier was the Rhine, although it had no interest in fielding a large army to help keep German troops on the eastern side. France was the only major land power capable of opposing German efforts for dominance; therefore, French security was important to Britain. Great Britain made no formal commitments to France, for fear of participation in another continental land war, but it did plan on committing its airpower and sea power to support France. Britain's primary European interest was the survival of French autonomy with its large land army.

Developing an offensive capability to conduct strategic air campaigns would serve to prevent the war Great Britain knew its empire could not afford. Avoiding the types of formal

44

strategic alliances it had before World War I would also help prevent involvement in another land war. The British Army would concentrate on the positive aim of preserving order within the colonies. Although the RAF would also help to control the colonies, it would focus its doctrine on ways to prevent an empire-wrecking war on the Continent. This doctrine would focus on defeating the enemy nation, perhaps a more efficient way to use airpower, but certainly a method to avoid engaging in land warfare.

Constraints to Strategy

Germany

Raw Materials

Germany possessed very few strategic natural resources and had to import most of the raw materials a war economy required. It had increased its dependence on imported raw materials since World War I and had insufficient reserves of every strategic raw material except coal, and the coal fields were in vulnerable border areas. Germany possessed 6 percent of the world's output of iron in 1938 and 2.9 percent of the output of bauxite, two raw materials crucial to an industrial-age military, especially an air force. It also depended on imports of nickel, tungsten, molybdenum, vanadium, and manganese, all components of high-grade steel. Without sufficient foreign exchange, Germany could not buy enough of these resources from other nations.[26]

Furthermore, Germany experienced critical shortages of raw materials during 1936 to 1938. These shortages, if not caused by, were certainly exacerbated by the widespread rearmament proceeding throughout all of Germany's armed forces. Labor and foreign exchange were also in short supply. These limitations would impact aircraft production negatively.

After his public announcement of the Luftwaffe's existence on 10 March 1935, Goering expected a steady annual increase of military aircraft production. However, after an increase up to 5,200 aircraft in 1936, production leveled off through 1938. Some of the factors causing this were outside the control of the Luftwaffe. The price of raw materials rose sharply at just the time Germany needed to increase its consumption. Foreign exchange did not increase because exporters could not expand sales abroad. Germany also needed to increase the importation of food. These factors forced Germany to conserve its foreign exchange resources.

The German air industry curtailed plant expansion and capital equipment purchases to make up for shortages of aluminum, iron, steel, cement, and wood. In 1937, the Luftwaffe cut production of aircraft by 25 percent, and the RLM cut the 1937 to 1938 budget by one billion reichmarks (RM) out of a 5.4 billion RM budget. Combat aircraft procurement was still the top priority, but it inevitably suffered. The emphasis on combat aircraft production was made at the expense of future capacity.[27]

Funding for rearmament was in short supply, causing the services to fight for money. The Luftwaffe reduced its funding to allow other services to modernize within the constraints of the enlarging industrial base and limited raw materials. After a rapid increase in aircraft production from 1933 to 1935, production reached a plateau of between 5,000 to 5,500 aircraft per year. This was also the period in which manufacturers were introducing in larger numbers the first generation of modern combat aircraft, the Bf 109, He 111, Do 17, and Ju 87. The Ju 88 was also under development as the eventual replacement for the He 111.[28] German industry was struggling to
match its ability to develop and produce mass quantities of aircraft with the requirements of the Luftwaffe.

A factor in deciding what type of aircraft to design and build was resources. Four-engine bombers required more material per unit produced than other types of aircraft. Even if the RLM could fund it, the contractors might not have enough of the material to actually build it in significant numbers.

Industrial / Technological Capabilities

A heavy bomber was the type of aircraft most suitable of carrying out the strategic

bombing role, as it was most capable of traveling the long distances to strike decisively at the

enemy's centers of power. Construction of such a bomber required the solution of several

technical problems. Effective heavy bombers required several qualities: speed, to increase

survivability; long range, to strike a distant enemy's centers of power; and the capability of flying

at high altitude, to evade many of the enemy's defenses. Powerful engines, accurate bombing

systems, and navigation and communication equipment were all crucial components of an

effective heavy bomber. These components had to be reliable enough for field units to use

regularly. They also had to be integrated into an effective airframe.[29]

The Chief of Air Command at the Air Ministry General Walter Wever authorized

Colonel Wimmer, the Chief of Technical Supply Department, to place an order for a four-engine

bomber in May 1934. The Do 19 and the Ju 89 were the resulting prototypes and were initially

the first developmental priority.[30] On 29 April 29 1937, Goering ordered work to be stopped on

these two programs at the request of Generals Milch and Kesselring. At the time, the aircraft

were limited to a speed of 175 knots and suitable engines were not immediately available.[31]

There is some dispute as to whether the aircraft would have been beneficial to the Luftwaffe had

it waited a few years until engines were available. Engines in the 600 to 700-horsepower class

equipped both aircraft, causing them to be underpowered. The adequacy of the designs if

equipped with 1,000-horsepower engines, when available, was a problem the leadership had to

contemplate. That issue might have been moot, considering the problems Germany had at that

time with raw materials. The Luftwaffe had also issued new guidelines on 17 April 1936,

endorsed by General Wever, which called for bombers with nearly double the range and speed

these prototypes would have been capable of achieving.[32]

After the Do 19 and Ju 89 were canceled, the Air Ministry tasked Heinkel to build a new

four-engine bomber, which became the He 177. The He 177 was designed to couple two engines to each propeller, minimizing drag while providing the necessary speed and range. The Air Ministry requirement to ensure it could perform dive-bombing, and problems with engine fires, limited its availability to combat units.[33] Germany was left with no viable heavy bomber.

The airframe industry was also a constraining factor in the production of modern military aircraft. The Air Ministry advocated licensing specific designs to other firms to increase capacity. However, poor coordination among the design and licensee firms reduced the effectiveness of this scheme. Faulty production programming was another problem, which the Air Ministry combated by using subcontractors. The expanding industry produced low quality aircraft relative to other national industries. The industry also continued to be plagued by a shortage of skilled workers, raw materials, and expansion capital.[34] The industry was gaining experience in mass-producing modern aircraft, but was still having problems with the basic requirements of fighters and twin-engine bombers. Heavy bombers would have compounded industry's problems.

Engines

Restrictions from the Treaty of Versailles and limitations on raw materials caused engine development to lag behind other industrial countries. Engine development was a chief bottleneck to the developing aircraft industry in interwar Germany. During World War I, Daimler Auto and Benz-Werke had made two-thirds of the air service's engines. After the war, Daimler concentrated on automobile engines and Benz-Werke gave up engine manufacturing, as it was in the demilitarized zone. In 1926, the two companies merged and resumed engine manufacturing. By 1933, only one-third of the Luftwaffe's engines in the 1,000-horsepower class were German-designed. The Army was a rival for engines, as the same manufacturers also built engines for combat vehicles.[35]

The low level of engine production in 1934 jeopardized the Rhineland Program of 1934 and 1935. Engine manufacturers required a different set of competencies and facilities than

48

airframe manufacturers, such as relying on precision machine shops, which made them harder to develop in a short period of time. Despite the effect the engine problems had on aircraft development, the Air Ministry decided it had to develop the German engine industry. It could not purchase engines from foreign companies due to Germany's lack of foreign exchange. Foreign governments were reluctant to license their best engines for German production. The Air Ministry knew that Germany needed to be self-sufficient in time of war. It also felt that the engine industry was starting to show promise.[36] The Air Ministry placed improvement of its domestic engine design and production ahead of fielding any particular type of aircraft, such as a heavy four-engine bomber.

Great Britain

A major constraint to the development of a British national military strategy to support its national strategy was the disparate aims of its militaries. Each service had a doctrine for a different threat. The army was geared for the duties of imperial police. The navy oriented itself toward Japan, the major threat to British colonies in Asia. The RAF concentrated on a potential threat from the Continent, France in the early 1920s but increasingly Germany. It desired to counter a potential German air offensive with a similar offensive. It also minimized its effort toward air defense and army support. Since Britain envisioned little role for the army in a large-scale land campaign, there was little incentive for the air force to do otherwise. The promise of swift and relatively cheap victories also contributed to the RAF's strategy.

After World War I, Britain perceived few major threats to its national security. As a budgetary measure, it assumed that a major war would be at least ten years in the future and budgeted for its military accordingly. The military budgets resulting from this "ten-year rule" produced a military incapable of executing its strategies, even the separate ones adhered to by the individual services.[37] When Germany and Italy appeared as threats to European stability in 1932, the ten-year rule was rescinded. However, military budgets were still very small, partly due to

49

the efforts of Neville Chamberlain, first as Chancellor of the Exchequer and then as Prime Minister.

Britain's intended strategy of deterrence through the threat of strategic bombing was constrained by the capabilities of the RAF. The specification leading to the first four-engine bomber was issued in 1936. Britain had done some excellent engine work, such as the initial version of the Rolls Royce Merlin in 1933. Aircrew capabilities were lacking, before World War II, the ability to fly at night and find their targets at night.[38] Thus Britain had the technological capability, but lacked compelling mission requirements and resources to fulfill its strategic air doctrine.

Conclusion

Germany's security environment and traditional military thought led it to plan for the execution of short, decisive wars dominated by ground warfare. It wanted to defeat its enemies quickly and sequentially in order to avoid a two-front war. It learned to employ aircraft as part of a combined arms team to achieve decisive victories. It also envisioned using its air force in deterrence and coercive roles. For it to be successful, it needed a large quantity of aircraft with which to influence its adversaries. Large numbers of fighters and small bombers were also a good fit for combined arms operations with the army. Given an aircraft industry that was recovering from disarmament, German leadership emphasized the production of larger numbers of medium bombers in preference to fewer numbers of four-engine bombers. The industry was also much more capable of producing twin-engine bombers because of experience and raw materials squeeze from 1936 to 1938.

Britain desired to refrain from war so that it could better maintain the balance of power in Europe and in its colonies. It chose its air force as a deterrence force, but through financial and training constraints evolved a force incapable of doing what it claimed it could do. Development of a strategic bombing doctrine also fit in with Britain's traditional detachment from continental land warfare and Britain's desire to threaten wars of attrition. Despite living in the same corner

of the world, Germany and Great Britain evolved different conceptions of airpower.

4 39

1

²Horst Boog, "Higher Command and Leadership in the German Luftwaffe, 1935-1945," in *Airpower and Warfare*, eds. Alfred C. Hurley and Robert C. Ehrhart (Washington, DC: U.S. Government Printing Office, 1979), 151.

³Hans Speier, "Ludendorff: The German Concept of Total War," in *Makers of Modern Strategy: Military Thought from Machiavelli to Hitler,* ed. Edward Mead Earle (Princeton, NJ: Princeton University Press, 1943; reprint, Princeton, NJ: Princeton University Press, 1971), 312-313.

⁴Boog, "Higher Command and Leadership in the German Luftwaffe, 1935-1945," 151.

⁵Barry R. Posen, *The Sources of Military Doctrine* (Ithaca, NY: Cornell University Press, 1984), 183, 190.

⁶Williamson Murray, "British and German Air Doctrine Between the Wars," *Air University Review* 31, no. 3 (1980): 41.

⁷Posen, 182; and Alan Robert Thoeny, "Role of the Separate Air Force in Nazi Germany" (Thesis, University of Wisconsin, 1963), 2.

⁸Friedrich Ruge, *Der Seekrieg: The German Navy's Story 1939-1945* (Annapolis, MD: United States Naval Institute, 1957), 25, 32-33; and Posen, 186.

⁹Hanfried Schliephake, *The Birth of the Luftwaffe* (London: Ian Allen Ltd., 1971), 38.

¹⁰Posen, 202-205.

¹¹Boog, "Higher Command and Leadership in the German Luftwaffe, 1935-1945," 150.

¹²Edward L. Homze, *Arming the Luftwaffe* (Lincoln, NE: University of Nebraska Press, 1976), 79.

¹³Homze, *Arming the Luftwaffe*, 55; Wilhelm Deist, *The Wehrmacht and German Rearmament* (Buffalo: University of Toronto Press, 1981), 54-57; and Klaus A. Maier, "Total War and German Air Doctrine Before the Second World War," in *The German*

Military in the Age of Total War, ed. Wilhelm Deist (Dover, NH: Berg Publishers, Ltd., 1985), 212-213.

[14]Posen, 194.

[15]David Irving, *The Rise and Fall of the Luftwaffe: The Life of Field Marshal Erhard Milch* (Boston: Little, Brown and Company, 1973), 55.

[16]Edward Mead Earle, "Hitler: The Nazi Concept of War," in *Makers of Modern Strategy: Military Thought from Machiavelli to Hitler,* ed. Edward Mead Earle (Princeton, NJ: Princeton University Press, 1943; reprint, Princeton, NJ: Princeton University Press 1971), 514; Richard Suchenwirth, *The Development of the German Air Force, 1919-1939* (New York: Arno Press, 1970), 188-190; and H. J. A. Wilson, "The Luftwaffe as a Political Instrument," in *The Impact of Air Power,* ed. Eugene M. Emme (Princeton, NJ: D. Van Nostrand Company, Inc., 1959), 60-61.

[17]Schliephake, 12-13.

[18]Homze, *Arming the Luftwaffe*, 2.

[19]Homze, *Arming the Luftwaffe*, 8-9; Schliephake, 18-26, 32. See also Wilhelm Speidel, "The Reichswehr's Illegal Air Force Command and its Secret Collaboration with Soviet Russia Before 1933," in *World War II German Military Studies,* vol. 23, eds. Donald S. Detwiler, Charles B. Burdick, and Jurgen Rohwer (New York: Garland Publishing, Inc., 1979), 1-151.

[20]Homze, *Arming the Luftwaffe*, 34-35.

[21]Schliephake, 34.

[22]Ibid., 48-50.

[23]Posen, 144.

[24]John Terraine, *The Right of the Line: The Royal Air Force in the European War 1939-1945* (Hertfordshire, UK: Wordsworth Editions Ltd., 1997), 30.

[25]Posen, 153-154.

[26]Williamson Murray, *The Change in the European Balance of Power, 1938-1939* (Princeton, NJ: Princeton University Press, 1984), 4-16.

[27]Edward L. Homze, "German Aircraft Production, 1918-1939," in *The Conduct of the Air War,* ed. Horst Boog (New York: Berg Publishers, 1992), 121-123.

[28]Edward L. Homze, "The Luftwaffe's Failure to Develop a Heavy Bomber Before World War II," *Aerospace Historian* 24, no. 1 (March 1977): 24.

[29]Homze, "German Aircraft Production, 1918-1939," 121.

[30]Homze, *Arming the Luftwaffe*, 122.

[31]Schliephake, 38-39.

[32]Homze, "The Luftwaffe's Failure," 22.

[33]Schliephake, 38-39; and Herbert Molloy Mason Jr., *The Rise of the Luftwaffe: Forging the Secret German Air Weapon 1918-1940* (New York: Dial Press, 1973), 257-259.

[34]Homze, *Arming the Luftwaffe*, 84.

[35]Ibid., 27-28.

[36]Ibid., 83.

[37]Posen, 146.

[38]Terraine, 17, 81-83.

CHAPTER 5

LEADERSHIP

The leadership of military organizations is ultimately the responsible party for adopting or revising doctrine. They are the people who are responsible for understanding lessons learned from past uses of military force, understanding the strategic setting and constraints, and developing a doctrine which is responsive to their nation's objectives and capabilities. This chapter will discuss the major leaders responsible for development of German Air Force doctrine, and those in positions to influence it. They will be compared to the effect leadership had on RAF doctrine.

Royal Air Force

The RAF was designated a separate service to combat the imminent threat of German bombing attacks in 1916 and 1917. After the war it needed to justify its existence as a separate service. Rivalry with the army and navy for missions and funding was a constant element of the political environment. The RAF needed a sense of purpose different from that of the army and navy to ensure funds from the Chancellor of the Exchequer. Trenchard's personality and leadership traits were crucial to maintaining an identity as a separate service.[1]

Trenchard

Hugh Trenchard was convinced airpower's proper role was to strike offensively at the enemy's sources of power to destroy its will to fight. In order to perform this task, he believed an independent service with control over a nation's entire air forces was crucial. While strategic bombing was important to Trenchard, its advocacy was perhaps even more important to the independent RAF.

One of Trenchard's methods to establish a lasting independent air force was the RAF Staff College at Andover. To Trenchard, one of the college's prime roles was a foundation for an RAF school of thought. He was primarily thinking of the concept of strategic bombing. The

RAF Operations Manual (CD 22) was one of the key instructional references. Trenchard and the staff consulted the first couple of classes to help the RAF formulate its basic doctrine. After that, the classes were on the receiving end of doctrine.

In addition to direct instruction, Trenchard and the college staff used two other methods to imbue doctrine to the RAF officers. From 1923 to 1928, the Air Ministry published outstanding airpower essays written by the students. The superiority of bombing's moral effects to its physical effects and the belief that the defensive use of fighters was a misuse of air resources were consistent points of view regarding airpower. Beginning in 1928, students also had to pass a written test. Students were expected to base their essay answers upon knowledge of official RAF doctrinal texts and readings recommended by the college. Essay answers to the tests were published along with the examiner's written responses. These publications ensured that all RAF officers knew the official doctrine.[2]

Trenchard used the Staff College as a tool to institutionalize support for the independent mission of strategic bombing. He also ensured that the best officers were assigned as instructors. The commandants at the staff college were chosen by Trenchard as were the instructors. These individuals bought into the efficacy of strategic bombing and promoted it to the students. Air Commodores Robert Brooke-Popham and Edgar Ludlow-Hewitt, the first two commandants, were both firm advocates of the power of strategic bombing. Ludlow-Hewitt later commanded Bomber Command from 1937 to 1940. Charles Portal and Arthur Tedder were also instructors before World War II who later became CAS.[3]

Trenchard was most effective working within the RAF to promote his views. As CAS, he was also in an authoritative position to ensure the doctrinal publications reflected his ideas on air warfare. Two such manuals were CD 22, *RAF Operations Manual,* published in 1922, and AP 1300, *The Royal Air Force War Manual*, published in July 1928.[4] The following chapter will discuss these two manuals further.

Through doctrinal publications and the staff college, Trenchard taught and institutionalized his views on strategic airpower. By World War II, they had become part of the RAF culture.

German Air Force

The Luftwaffe's leadership before and during World War II had many differences from that of the RAF. The RAF had continuity and the staff college to develop a school of thought concerning airpower. The Luftwaffe was composed of officers who transferred from the army with recent operational and staff experience: Wever, Kesselring, Wilberg, and Jeschonnek; and a number who had been away from the military for some time, such as Goering, Udet, and Milch. The high-ranking officers with World War I experience were fighter pilots, not bomber pilots with strategic air warfare experience.[5]

The Army transferred 200 officers to the Luftwaffe in 1933. These officers were first-class leaders, including Kesselring, Stumpf, and Wever. They did have a firm understanding of basic army requirements and sound military traditions. However, the new officers did not include Ernst Brandenburg, the senior World War I bomber pilot.[6] The Luftwaffe did not enjoy the same leadership continuity and medium, the staff college, through which to indoctrinate large numbers of officers with theory and doctrine that the RAF employed so well.

Hitler

Adolf Hitler became the Chancellor of Germany in January 1933. As a result of several organizational changes, he assumed the role of Supreme Commander of Armed Forces in the new Oberkommando der Wehrmacht (OKW) in 1938, replacing Field Marshal Werner Von Blomberg's former authority as Minister of War.

Adolf Hitler was Germany's political as well as its military leader and his successes in Austria, Czechoslovakia, and the Ruhr were achieved partly through the apparent strength of the Luftwaffe. His major interest in the Luftwaffe during rearmament was to build as large an air force as possible so that it could be used as a coercive tool for accomplishing national strategic objectives, like seizing the Sudetenland and Austria. This was consistent with his appreciation of airpower as a political rather than economic weapon. Later in the war he pushed for V-1 and V-2 deployment to terrorize the will of the British people rather than attacking its munitions industry. This was in marked contrast to Luftwaffe doctrine, which advocated attacks on munitions industries and not on populations. In the end, his advocacy of combining aircraft and armor for blitzkrieg may have been a factor in pushing Luftwaffe procurement toward dive-bombers and medium bombers.[7] However, the greatest effect he had on its doctrinal development may be what he did not do. He steered the German military services toward preparation for wars against Poland, Czechoslovakia, and France. He may have wanted to avoid fighting Great Britain early in his reign, but when the situation changed, he did not forcefully make this known to the air force. The same could be said concerning the Soviet Union. If the RLM had planned for an attack on either Great Britain or the Soviet Union or both, its procurement decisions might have been different. Hitler was a factor in ensuring that Germany had an independent air force, but his beliefs were inconsistent with published Luftwaffe doctrine written by professional officers.

Hermann Goering

> At the start of the war Germany was the only country in the world to have a strategic air force with machines that were absolutely modern from the technical point of view. The other states had split their air force into an army air force and a navy air force, and above all considered the air force as a necessary and important adjunct to the two other services. For that reason they lacked that instrument which alone can deliver concentrated and shattering blows -- the strategic air force. In Germany we worked from the start on lines that the main body of the Luftwaffe should fly deep into the enemy's country and operate
>
> strategically, while a detached portion should primarily appear on the battlefield as dive bombers or, of course fighters.[8]

Werner Baumbach, *The Life and Death of the Luftwaffe*

Speaking in 1943, Hermann Goering no doubt felt his Luftwaffe was strategic, or perhaps he confused "strategic" with "separate." At any rate, he was the most visible leader of the

German Air Force and is most popularly identified with its accomplishments and doctrine. While he was the Air Minister and Commander in Chief of the German Air Force, he also wore many other political titles: Prime Minister of Prussia, President of the Reichstag, Chief Game Warden of the Reich, Master of Forestry, and Economic Controller of the German Four Year Plan[9]

Goering's Air Ministry title, assumed in 1933, was a cabinet-level position, on par with the war minister, then-Colonel General Werner von Blomberg. The Air Ministry had civilian functions and at the time performed as the front for the still-secret air force. When the Luftwaffe was announced in 1935, Goering became its commander as well. This situation made him equal with the war minister on the cabinet, but subordinate in theory to him as head of the air force, resulting in de facto independence from other services at the highest command levels.[10]

Goering's major influence over doctrinal development was his political influence that ensured the establishment of an independent air force. On 26 February 1935, Hitler signed a decree making the Air Force the third independent military, effective 1 March 1935. The air force was to be known as the Reichsluftwaffe, shortened quickly to Luftwaffe.[11] Hitler's intent was political, as much as military. He wanted to ensure that his top assistant, Goering, had an important base of power within the Third Reich.[12] Goering quickly rose to Colonel General (*Generaloberst*) on 1 April 1936 and Field Marshal on 4 February 1938. Under Goering, the air force was free to develop doctrine without influence from army commanders, or perhaps, Goering himself. This may have been just as well. He had too many responsibilities and too many other interests to give consistent guidance.[13] He later claimed to work primarily out of his offices in the Prussian State Ministry rather than the Air Ministry.[14]

This is not to say Goering's leadership was ineffective. His personality often inspired the air force to accomplish great efforts during its buildup. He did lead the Luftwaffe's growth from a very small organization. He was also credited with being a follower of Douhet's principles.

However, he was handicapped by his loss of touch with aviation technology during the 1920s. He was not a major influence on published doctrine.[15]

General Hans von Seeckt

> When we speak of the technical side of modern warfare, we think first of all of the aerial arm. During the war -- and still more since -- this branch assumed a position of equality with the land and sea forces, without changing the fundamental laws of war.[16]
>
> General Hans von Seeckt, *Thoughts of a Soldier*

A study of leadership influences on the German Air Force has to include General Hans von Seeckt. Von Seeckt served in the eastern front during World War I against Russia and with Turkey. In 1919, he was head of the *Truppenamt*, or troops office, the de facto General Staff, later serving as commander of the German Army until October 1926. He viewed the Versailles Treaty as an obstacle to be overcome, and emphasized quality with his 100,000-man army. His immediate goal was to prepare Germany to fight a war against the most probable enemy, Poland.

Von Seeckt placed a high importance on aviation after the war, ensuring that 180 experienced flying officers were distributed throughout the Reichswehrministerium (RWM), the German war ministry. He did envision an independent air force in Germany's future. To further this aim, he helped cultivate ties with Russia, leading to German aviators training in the Soviet Union.[17]

Von Seeckt perceived that two failures of the German Army during World War I were its inability to prevent French mobilization and the failure to prevent French redeployment. He thought aircraft could provide answers. He believed that aviation's first priority was the destruction of the enemy air force by surprise attack when it was on the ground. When the command of the air was ensured, air forces were to disrupt enemy mobilization by attacking troop concentrations at the front and immediately behind it. He did not see a role for air forces in attacking the enemy's economy or population.[18] He stated "destruction of the enemy's army, not destruction of the country, remains the supreme law of war."[19] His idea of future warfare was epitomized by the employment of mobile armies rendered more effective by aircraft.

Von Seeckt envisioned an important role for aviation in future warfare, although different from that of Douhet. Aided by his eastern front experience, he also saw ground warfare differently, thinking in terms of mobile rather than static defensive battles. His greatest contribution to the future Luftwaffe was his preservation of staff officers in the *Truppenamt* to study airpower theory and develop future doctrine. Major Helmut Wilberg was among the officers he retained.

Erhard Milch

Milch was an army officer during World War I and subsequently a leader of the German national airline Lufthansa. He became State Secretary of the Air Ministry in 1933, subordinate only to Goering. Concerning views on air doctrine, Milch did not emphasize strategic bombing. According to a memo he wrote to Goering in 1936, the Luftwaffe's task should be to attack the enemy air force and support the army and navy.[20] In his billet, Milch was not responsible for air doctrine, but did have responsibilities for resourcing the air force, and implementing the doctrine. He was part of the power structure within the air ministry. After Wever's death, he played a part in the power struggles with Kesselring, Stumpf, and Jeschonnek. These power struggles only served to confuse the chain of command and could not help the Luftwaffe address its resource requirements adequately.

During testimony at Nuremberg, Milch allowed that the four-engine prototypes, the Do 19 and Ju 89, were technically suitable. He testified that they were canceled due to their large expense and the perceived lack of an impending war. There were also not enough reserves or domestic production of aluminum, magnesium, rubber to support a four-engine bomber program. Upon a recommendation from the Chief of Staff, Kesselring, he stopped production of the four-engine aircraft. Goering also approved this action. No matter why it was canceled, its absence

limited the scope and range of the German bomber forces.

General Walther Wever

General Wever transferred from the Reichswehr to the Air Ministry and became chief of

the Air Command Office on 1 September 1933. He was billeted as the future chief of the

Luftwaffe General Staff. Although an infantry officer, he learned to fly and ensured that other

leaders new to the air ministry did as well. He soon became an advocate for an independent air

force spearheaded by strategic bombers. Many of his contemporaries classified him as a genius

on the level of Moltke.[21]

General Wever placed great importance on the creation of a strong bomber force and saw

the Soviet Union as Germany's most serious threat. He had read *Mein Kampf* and followed

Hitler's inclination towards the Soviet Union as the major source of conflict. Important targets

would be Soviet industry east of the Ural Mountains. He tasked the Technical Office to develop a

four-engine bomber, referring to it as the "Ural Bomber." With these bombers, he could destroy

weapons in factories up to 1,500 miles distant from German bases.[22]

Wever knew the air force could bypass traditional boundaries. With the air force, he

envisioned avoiding the static defensive fight of the Western Front of World War I. The aircraft

would be an important element in mobile warfare. His core belief concerning air warfare was

that it was part of a larger plan. Air warfare would play a significant part and may even play a

strategic part, but would not be separate from the overall battle. Priorities were the destruction of

the enemy's air force, his army, navy, sources of supply, and the armament industry. In a war

against Great Britain, Wever felt that strategic bombers would play a decisive role against Great

Britain through attacks on its industry and maritime strength. War games in 1936 even included

attacks on political and military targets in Prague in a simulated war against Czechoslovakia[23]

Wever was in favor of a balanced doctrine. He emphasized defense from air attack using active defense and passive defense. He argued for cooperation and coordination of defending fighters and antiaircraft artillery.

Defense was important, but attack was the decisive task for the air force. The first priority was destruction of the enemy's air forces, including at the factory. Next was the prevention of large enemy ground forces massing at decisive points, disruption of enemy armored forces, participation in naval battles, and paralysis of the enemy through attack on the enemy factories.[24] These tasks were similar to von Seeckt's, but Wever also included attacks on industry. He maintained that victory would be achieved by defeating the enemy's military forces.

> The objective of any war is to destroy the morale of the enemy. The morale of a leader and of a nation is reflected to a great extent in the armed forces of that nation. Thus, in a war of the future, the destruction of the armed forces will be of primary importance. This can mean: the destruction of the enemy air force, army, and navy, and of the source of supply of the enemy's forces: the armament industry. The point at which concentrated use will be made of the air force at any given time will be decided by the situation as a whole.[25]

One of Wever's strengths was his leadership ability within the air ministry. He was able to work with Goering and Milch, two very different personalities. His death on 3 June 1936 would reduce the effectiveness of the Luftwaffe staff, as well as rob it of an effective leader.[26] Before he died, however, he sponsored the publication of the last major doctrinal publication written by the Luftwaffe before World War II, Luftwaffe Regulation 16: *Luftkriegführung* (The Conduct of the Air War), referred to as LF 16, which incorporated his conception of airpower.

Helmut Wilberg

Wilberg was an experienced pilot during World War I. He had commanded army level aviation forces, including as many as 700 aircraft. Von Seeckt knew him and picked him as his air advisor during the Versailles Treaty negotiations in 1919. After the war, he commanded the air organization and training office. He was an active part of the effort to study aviation in the recent war as well as aviation in foreign air forces.

In 1926, he was part of a committee that published *Directives for the Conduct of the Operational Air War*.[27] He was a major general in 1933 when the Air Ministry was reforming a unified air force, and may have been the logical choice to be its chief of staff. His combat record was excellent and his study and development after that were crucial. However, as his mother was Jewish, command was not in his future under the Nazi leadership. Wilberg was assigned to chair the committee that Wever assigned to write a new doctrinal publication. This publication became Luftwaffe Regulation 16.[28]

Successors to Wever

Wever presided over the Luftwaffe staff when it published its last major doctrine prior to World War II. His successors did not significantly change the doctrine, but their procurement and training decisions influenced how it was implemented.

Udet

Ernst Udet was the leading surviving ace from World War I, with sixty-two victories. He was known to Goering and Hitler for his flying expertise, not his technical abilities. He had studied the US Navy's use of dive-bombers and was intrigued by their accuracy. After Wever's death, Udet became the Chief of the Technical Office, replacing Colonel Wimmer.

Udet influenced both Goering and Kesselring on the capabilities of the dive-bomber. His arguments were backed up by the experience of the Condor Legion in Spain. The Ju 87 *Stukas* had proven capable of hitting targets precisely. The medium bombers were not used to hit strategic level targets, but concentrated on interdiction.[29]

His belief in the dive-bomber went beyond the Ju 87. The Technical Office issued orders requiring subsequent medium and heavy bombers to be capable of dive-bombing. This was for both accuracy and survivability. This order impacted the Ju 88, a follow-on medium bomber, and the next four-engine bomber, the He 177.[30] Udet may have had some solid evidence concerning the efficiency of dive-bombing, but its application to large bomber aircraft had negative

consequences for their production, and application of the published doctrine.

Kesselring

General Albert Kesselring served in the Bavarian Army as an artillery officer during

World War I. He continued in the Reichswehr after the war in various staff and command billets.

His leadership and administrative abilities gained him recognition and made him valuable for the

new air arm when it needed an influx of competent officers in 1933. He assumed duties as Chief

of the Luftwaffe General Staff on 15 August 1936, serving until 30 May 1937.[31]

Kesselring agreed the air force was an offensive arm. He believed attacks should be

limited to strictly military targets and prohibited attacks on open towns and civilians. Being a

former army staff officer, he understood well the needs of the army, and believed the aircraft

could also be used well in close support of ground forces.

He did not share with Douhet and other air theorists the belief that air forces alone could

defeat an enemy. He felt that Germany could only bring war with England to an end through

invasion. He was comfortable that Germany had prepared well for warfare against its neighbors,

but was unable to build a truly offensive air force complete with long-range four engine bombers

capable of striking deeper into Great Britain or the Soviet Union. Germany possessed the

fighters, medium bombers, and dive-bombers essential for waging war against its most probable

enemies, neighboring France, Poland, and Czechoslovakia.[32]

While Kesselring was Chief of Staff, the Condor Legion was formed to support

Generalissimo Franco's rebellion in Spain. The Luftwaffe provided fighter, ground support, and

bomber units and acquired experience in the tactical and operational levels of air warfare. It

learned how to be proficient at air-to-air warfare and at coordinating operations with the ground

forces.

Kesselring had a difficult time maintaining effective working relationships with other senior leaders, notably Erhard Milch. This influenced his desire to resign as Chief of Staff in 1937. However, he did agree with Milch on the infeasibility of the "Ural Bomber" program, under which the prototypes Do 19 and Ju 89 were built. Factors including shortages of raw materials, inadequate manufacturing capacity, long-range aerial navigation and target acquisition, and the lack of foreseeable political necessity all contributed to their positions. At the time, they envisaged hostilities beginning sometime between 1941 and 1943.[33]

Kesselring did not change the doctrine published by Wever. However, he participated in decisions that directly affected the Luftwaffe's ability to execute the doctrine against specific countries, namely Great Britain and the Soviet Union.

Jeschonnek

After General Hans-Jurgen Stumpf, General Hans Jeschonnek became Chief of Staff, and led the Luftwaffe through 1943. In July 1932 he had been an advocate for centralization of all aviation forces under the defense ministry. Although the senior leadership did not immediately act on his memorandum, it was one stimulus leading to an independent air force. Kesselring evaluated Jeschonnek as an above average general and thought he was capable of defending his views with Goering and Hitler.[34]

Jeschonnek's impact on strategic air doctrine was similar to that of Udet's. He advocated dive-bombing as an essential characteristic for bomber aircraft. He considered dive-bombing a form of precision weapon. Germany's resource challenges forced a trend toward creating the greatest possible effects with the least number of aircraft and ordnance. He did intend some type of strategic warfare by using aircraft such as the Ju 87 to perform accurate attacks on targets like power plants. Unlike Wever, he did not anticipate a war with the Soviet Union, so aircraft with shorter ranges were appropriate.[35]

Conclusions

65

Great Britain entered World War II identifying strategic air warfare as its prime air mission. Trenchard's leadership was a major reason. He had identified his theories for the proper employment of airpower. The postwar environment threatened the existence of an independent air service through the pressure of funding. Trenchard used the role of strategic airpower as a distinct mission for airpower to advance his aim for preserving an independent service. He also used the institution of the RAF, especially its staff college, to provide a continuity of thought the German Air Force was unable to experience. Through his leadership and that of his successors, he was able to institutionalize the concept of strategic bombing in the RAF.

Germany experienced different leadership influences than Great Britain, in part due to the Treaty of Versailles. Von Seeckt as the commander of the army was able to advocate an independent air arm without the implications of budgets. Through study and analysis, he employed former air officers from World War I, such as Helmuth Wilberg to study and write doctrines for a future German air force. When Hitler and Goering seized power, the seed was planted for a doctrine that included strategic air warfare. Hitler and Goering provided the firm political base for an independent air force and the money to build it. The stimulus for building the force structure existed through the desire to deter foreign interference with German rearmament and to coerce neighbors into acquiescing to Hitler's aims. General Wever, perhaps the finest leader the Luftwaffe had, sponsored a doctrine that advocated aspects of strategic air doctrine similar to Douhet, but not as a completely independent offensive. The leadership failings of the Luftwaffe leadership, including Hitler, negatively impacted the ability to implement its doctrine by failing to prepare for the proper adversaries (Great Britain and the Soviet Union), misapplying technology (dive-bombing), and inadequately managing production and aircraft design (the Ju 89, Do 19, and the He 177). The influence of these two leaders helped ensure that strategic air doctrine became a part, but not the dominant part of German air operations.

66

[1]Richard J. Overy, "Doctrine not Dogma: Lessons From the Past," *The Royal Air Force Air Power Review* 3, no. 1 (spring 2000): 37.

[2]Allan D. English, "The RAF Staff College and the Evolution of Strategic Bombing Policy, 1922-1929," *The Journal of Strategic Studies* 16, no. 3 (September 1993): 408-419.

[3]Ibid., 410-415.

[4]Phillip S. Meilinger, "Trenchard, Slessor, and Royal Air Force Doctrine Before World War II," in *The Paths of Heaven: The Evolution of Airpower Theory,* ed. Phillip S. Meilinger (Maxwell Air Force Base, AL: Air University Press, 1997), 53-56; and Sir Charles Webster and Noble Frankland, *The Strategic Air Offensive Against Germany 1939-1945,* vol. 4 (London: Her Majesty's Stationery Office, 1961), 71-76.

[5]Horst Boog, "Higher Command and Leadership in the German Luftwaffe, 1935-1945," in *Airpower and Warfare,* eds. Alfred C. Hurley and Robert C. Ehrhart (Washington DC: U.S. Government Printing Office, 1979), 134-135.

[6]Matthew Cooper, *The German Air Force 1933-1945, An Anatomy of Failure* (London: Jane's Publishing Company Ltd., 1981), 6.

[7]Richard J. Overy, "Hitler and Air Strategy," *Journal of Contemporary History* 15 (1980): 405-411.

[8]Werner Baumbach, *The Life and Death of the Luftwaffe* (New York: Ballantine Books, 1949), 47. Goering was speaking on 8 November 1943 to a group of Reichs Commissioners.

[9]Asher Lee, *The German Air Force* (New York: Harper and Brothers Publishers, 1946), 6.

[10]Telford Taylor, *Sword and Swastika: Generals and Nazis in the Third Reich* (New York: Simon and Schuster, 1952), 107-108.

[11]Cooper, 4.

[12]Overy, "Hitler and Air Strategy," 406.

[13]Taylor, 107-109.

[14]Headquarters Air P/W Interrogation Detachment, Military Intelligence Service, 9th Air Force, *Enemy Intelligence Summaries, Hermann Goering.* (Military Intelligence Service, 9th Air Force, 1 June 1945), 5.

[15]James S. Corum, "The Development of Strategic Air War Concepts in Interwar Germany, 1919-1939," *Air Power History* 44, no. 4 (winter 1997): 27; and Richard Suchenwirth, *The Development of the German Air Force, 1919-1939* (New York: Arno Press, 1970), 54-55.

[16]General von Seeckt, *Thoughts of a Soldier,* trans. Gilbert Waterhouse (London: Ernest Benn Ltd., 1930), 59-60.

[17]Taylor, 28-30.

[18]Larry H. Addington, *The Blitzkrieg Era and the German General Staff, 1865-1941* (New Brunswick, NJ: Rutgers University Press, 1971), 29-30.

[19]von Seeckt, 59.

[20]Manfred Messerschmidt, "German Military Effectiveness Between 1919 and 1939," in *Military Effectiveness,* vol. 2, *The Interwar Period,* eds. Allan R. Millett and Williamson Murray (Winchester, MA: Unwin Hyman, Inc., 1988), 247.

[21]Edward L. Homze, *Arming the Luftwaffe* (Lincoln, NE: University of Nebraska Press, 1976), 59-60; Andreas Nielsen, *The German Air Force General Staff* (New York: Arno Press, 1968), 28; and Suchenwirth, *The Development of the German Air Force, 1919-1939,* 59.

[22]Nielsen, 172; Herbert Molloy Mason Jr., *The Rise of the Luftwaffe: Forging the Secret German Air Weapon 1918-1940* (New York: Dial Press, 1973), 185; and Richard Suchenwirth, *Command and Leadership in the German Air Force* (New York: Arno Press, 1970), 5-6.

[23]Mason, 185; and Suchenwirth, *Command and Leadership in the German Air Force,* 12.

[24]Major General Max Wever, "Doctrine of the German Air Force," in *The Impact of Air Power,* ed. Eugene M. Emme (Princeton, NJ: D. Van Nostrand Company, Inc., 1959), 184-185.

[25]Ibid., 184.

[26]Kenneth Macksey, *Kesselring: The Making of the Luftwaffe* (New York: David McKay Company, Inc., 1978), 48.

[27]James S. Corum, *The Luftwaffe: Creating the Operational Air War, 1918-1940* (Lawrence, KS: The University Press of Kansas, 1997), 81-83.

[28]Ibid., 125-127.

[29]Addington, 44.

[30]Suchenwirth, *Command and Leadership in the German Air Force*, 82.

[31]Albert Kesselring, *The Memoirs of Field Marshall Kesselring,* trans. William Kimber (Bonn: Athenaum, 1953; reprint, Novato, CA: Presidio Press, 1989), 25-26; and Macksey, 47-53.

[32]International Military Tribunal, *Trial of the Major War Criminals Before the International Military Tribunal, Nuremburg 14 November 1945 - 1 October 1946,* vol. 9 (Nuremburg: International Military Tribunal, 1947), 203-207.

[33]Macksey, 51-52.

[34]Homze, *Arming the Luftwaffe,* 48; and Kesselring, 44.

[35]Suchenwirth, *The Development of the German Air Force, 1919-1939,* 95-96, 153-154; and Suchenwirth, *Command and Leadership in the German Air Force,* 226.
[36]

CHAPTER 6

PREWAR STRATEGIC AIR DOCTRINE

The Royal Air Force and the Luftwaffe published a series of doctrinal manuals

throughout the 1920s and 1930s. These manuals summarized each organization's fundamental

beliefs regarding how it could best contribute toward winning each nation's projected wars.

These doctrines represent culmination of the factors discussed in the previous chapters and

displayed each air force's "finalized" maturity as their nations moved toward war.

Royal Air Force

The RAF's Air Staff entered World War II with a conviction that the proper role for an

air force was to aim for a decisive moral effect by bombing military objectives within populated

areas, even in place of pursuing air superiority. They advocated this strategy even while they

recognized that history showed that air superiority should be achieved first.[1]

CD 22

CD 22, the *RAF Operations Manual*, was its first doctrinal manual and was published in

July 1922. It reflected Trenchard's views on the importance of coordinating air operations with

the army. The objective of the air force was still the defeat of the enemy's main forces in

coordination with the ground forces. The manual did consider morale to be a crucial component

to air warfare. One side achieved victory when it imposed enough pressure on the enemy's

population to force its government to seek peace.[2]

CD 22 regarded air superiority as the key prerequisite to achieving other objectives.

Once air superiority was assured, the bomber force was free to conduct offensive operations

against sources of power related to military objectives. The manual listed naval bases, munitions

factories, and railway junctions as suitable targets. These targets were also related to a nation's

military sources of power. Attacks on legitimate targets in population centers were allowed as

long as reasonable precautions were taken to prevent damage to places such as hospitals.[3]

AP 1300, July 1928

AP 1300, *The Royal Air Force War Manual*, published in July 1928, was consistent with

the 1922 version concerning the primacy of the offensive, the moral value of airpower and the use

of the air force in a joint role toward the defeat of the enemy's armed forces.[4] It reflected

Trenchard's evolving views on the role of the air force, as well as of the armed forces, as

expressed in his memorandum to the Chiefs of Staff Sub-Committee on the War Object of an Air

Force, dated 2 May 1928. He felt the role of all the services was "to defeat the enemy nation, not

merely its army, navy or air force."[5]

Although important, air superiority was no longer a prerequisite to conducting the

strategic bombing campaign. Air superiority need not be established before proceeding to bomb

enemy sources of power. Emphasizing air superiority might result in accomplishing nothing else.

The objectives of a strategic bombing campaign were wider and aimed to affect more

than the military sources of power. The bombing objectives depended on "the nature of the war

and the enemy; the general war plan of the government; diplomatic considerations; the range of

the bombers; and the strength of the enemy air defenses." Bombardment objectives should

weaken the enemy's resistance and his overall ability to continue the war. These objectives might

include the enemy's vital centers including production, supply, communications, and

transportation systems. Disrupting these centers could be more effective than assisting the army

or navy.[6]

The manual continued to state that victory resulted from the collapse of civilian morale.

As Trenchard had stated, this collapse would occur by disrupting the workers' lives through

bombardment of their livelihoods, the munitions factories and other vital centers.[7] He did not

envision bombardment of the population's living areas itself.

As Trenchard wrote to his fellow service chiefs concerning RAF doctrine in May 1928:

In pursuit of this objective, air attacks will be directed against any objectives which will contribute effectively towards the destruction of the enemy's means of resistance and the lowering of his determination to fight.

These objectives will be military objectives. Among these will be comprised the enemy's great centres of production of every type of war material, from battleships to boots, his essential munition factories, the centres of all his systems of communications and transportation, his docks and shipyards, railway workshops, wireless stations, and postal and telegraph systems.[8]

Role of population bombing

The RAF firmly believed that strategic bombing could bring victory by collapsing civilian morale. However, it did not officially sanction bombing population centers to create terror. Trenchard emphatically distinguished between bombings that might harm civilians engaged in building armaments and indiscriminate bombings that would terrorize the entire population of a city. He was not alone. Air Commodore Ludlow-Hewitt, commander of Bomber Command at the beginning of World War II, and Wing Commander Arthur Tedder both stated in their air staff college lectures that population bombing was inhuman and military ineffective in their air staff college lectures.[9]

AP 1300, February 1940

A new edition of *The Royal Air Force War Manual* was published just after the beginning of World War II, although it was written before the war started. It reflected RAF planning for a possible conflict with Germany, which it had recognized as a potential adversary by the time it began its rearmament program in 1935.

Under this latest manual, offensive action continued to be the main goal of an air force, and the objective of this offensive action was to defeat the enemy's national will. The enemy will was embodied by its armed forces, manpower, economic power, and financial power. Military forces were to either defeat the enemy's military forces, conduct an economic blockade, or disrupt the enemy people's normal lives to make them war weary. The manual stated that the true purpose for an air force was to disrupt the enemy people's normal lives.

Bombing attacks should focus on enemy industry and infrastructure, such as public utilities, food and fuel supplies, and transportation and communication networks. These attacks would be designed to disrupt the normal lives of the enemy population and induce war weariness among it.[10]

The RAF did not foresee a close relationship with the army. The air staff was vocal about not using bombers on the battlefield. The closest that bomber support would get to the battlefield would be to isolate the enemy's armies from resupply and reinforcement, and to create disruption and confusion behind the enemy's front, much like air interdiction.[11]

Again, as represented in the first AP 1300, the RAF did not subscribe to area bombing to terrorize population centers. Bombers were to be given specific targets in the oil, gas, transportation, aircraft, and iron industries, among others, the destruction or damage of which was calculated to cause particular effects to the enemy's ability to resist. The manual's writers assumed the ability to precisely locate and target these point targets.[12]

The planning done by the Air Staff's Plans Division for a possible war with Germany was consistent with its doctrine. Several Western Air (W.A.) plans were developed beginning in 1937. The most prominent offensive bombing plans were W.A. 1, W.A. 4, and W.A. 5. W.A. 1 aimed at destroying the German offensive air capability through attacks on its forces and aircraft industry. W.A. 4 included attacks on German military rail, road, and canal communications to interdict ground force concentrations. W.A. 5 was an attack on the German war and oil industries.[13]

The RAF intended to defeat the enemy nation by attacking its will to fight. Attacks on the enemy's economic, military, and political sources of power, with emphasis on the economic power, would significantly disrupt the enemy's life and cause the population to force the government to seek peace.

Luftwaffe

Directives for the Execution of the Operational Air War

During his tour as senior air officer of the Reichswehr, Lieutenant Colonel Helmuth Wilberg and his staff wrote a doctrine for the use of a future German air force. At this time German aviators were conducting clandestine training in the Soviet Union, but Germany was several years away from standing up established military aviation units. The *Directives for the Execution of the Operational Air War* was published in May 1926 and based on the staff's study of foreign air forces and theorists, as well as lessons from World War I. The lack of a force structure precluded the execution of such a doctrine within the foreseeable future.

A future German air force would be separate, but would not necessarily act independently from the other services. The high command would decide the nature of the operational air war, and even decide if the air force would be able to conduct an operational air war. The conception of an operational air war in this doctrine had elements similar to strategic air warfare, in that attacks would be conducted against targets in the enemy's homeland to defeat an enemy's ability to wage war.[14]

The doctrine discussed the ability of air forces to bypass ground and naval forces to attack the "innermost political, moral, economic, and military sources of power of a state." The air force would direct its attacks against the population, industry, transportation net, and enemy armed forces and supporting facilities. These attacks would be designed to "crush the enemy's moral resistance and will to fight by targeting his armaments industry and food distribution."[15] Doctrinally, a future German air force could conduct strategic attacks on an enemy's economic, moral, and military sources of strength.

This document did not dictate which sources of power should be targeted:

> The supreme military commander must be in accord with the national leadership in deciding whether the attack is preferred against political targets, the basis for the population's will to resist, or against the enemy war industry -- the source of power for the armed forces.[16]

74

The doctrine did identify specific sources of power that would have significant effects--the enemy's vital centers. The armament industry was the key to attacking the enemy's military source of power. The power industry was the key to the enemy's civil life and economy. Attacks on the enemy's major power generators would have significant effects on the enemy's economy, war industry and moral resistance. Enemy seaports were the key targets to attack in order to prevent the enemy from deploying its combat power against friendly forces.[17]

Air superiority was identified as the major role for the air force. Ideally it should be pursued through attacks on the enemy's peacetime airfields, if possible. If not, attacks of the mobilization bases, and air depots, factories, and training bases would be used. The manual was skeptical of efforts to achieve command of the air through defensive operations.[18]

The manual envisioned that the decisive battle would be a ground battle. Upon the approach of this battle, the air force was to concentrate its efforts on attacking the enemy's armed forces and their systems of supply. Concentration of effort was emphasized, because it would achieve the greatest effect. This might dictate a diminished effort against the enemy's sources of power to facilitate a more successful decisive battle.

Luftwaffe Regulation 16

General Wever directed the writing of an operational air doctrine for the new Luftwaffe in 1934. Major General Wilberg led the air ministry staff that responded to this requirement and wrote *Luftwaffe Dienstvorschrift* 16, *Luftkriegfuhrung* (Luftwaffe Regulation 16: *The Conduct of the Aerial War*), publishing it in 1935.[19] It stressed the offensive nature of air warfare and the importance of carrying the war to the enemy. In addition to discussing functions that supported the other services, it emphasized functions that advanced air force independence, such as strategic attacks and air superiority. The Luftwaffe did not assert that the air force alone could decide the outcome of war.[20]

The manual envisioned the operation of the air force within a combined environment.

(The term "combined" was used to mean multi-service, similar to the term "joint.") The decision

of what missions the air force would prosecute would be made by the combined commander, not

the air commander, although some missions were certainly deemed essential, like air superiority.

Many air leaders felt the proper role for an independent air force was to assist advancing ground

forces by removing the enemy's air threat.[21]

Similar to the RAF in the late 1930s, the Luftwaffe stated the mission of the armed forces

was to break down the will of the enemy. However, the Luftwaffe identified the will of the

nation differently. "The will of the nation finds its greatest embodiment in its armed forces."

Therefore the primary goal for the Luftwaffe and the other services was the destruction of the

enemy armed forces.[22]

Paragraph 10 identified three specified tasks for the Luftwaffe in time of war: air

superiority; joint operations; and strategic operations. These tasks were to be accomplished

within a framework of joint operations:

> By battling the enemy air force, the enemy armed forces are weakened, and, at
> the same time, our own armed forces, our people, and our homeland are protected.
> By taking part in operations and conflict on land and at sea, the Luftwaffe
> directly supports the army and navy.
> By fighting directly against the sources of power of the enemy armed forces and
> by breaking down the flow of support from the homeland to the front, the enemy armed
> forces can also be brought to defeat.[23]

Air superiority was the primary role for the Luftwaffe. The Luftwaffe was to maintain a

persistent campaign even after initial air superiority was gained. The battle for air superiority was

to be directed at the enemy's air fighting units initially. Assuming success, subsequent air

superiority objectives would be the enemy air force's supply, personnel replacement, and aircraft

production centers.[24] Air superiority would be gained through a combination of counterforce and

strategic attack methodologies.

The combined war leadership would decide when the air force would conduct operations in direct support of the army and navy. The manual recognized that the air superiority fight would continue during direct support missions. It also believed that other targets farther in the enemy rear might be more effective than direct support and that the air force should continue attacks against these sources of power. The air component commander could also be assigned to an army supreme command or army staff to promote effective air support for the army.[25]

The Luftwaffe theorists postulated that attacks on the enemy sources of power were the most effective role for the air force. These attacks would focus on sources of power used to supply and support the enemy armed forces, including production facilities, food production, import facilities, power stations, railroads and rail yards, military barracks, and centers of government administration. Some of these targets were also sources of power for the civilian economy, but the Luftwaffe targeted them for the purpose of hurting the enemy armed forces.[26]

Unlike Douhet, the manual asserts that these strategic attacks were a slow method to defeat the enemy, and might not influence the military and naval campaigns in sufficient time to be decisive. These attacks were more appropriate for a long war.[27] The authors recognized that Germany's military leaders had long ago concluded that a long war was not in the national interest. Air superiority and operations in support of the army and navy were thus given higher priority than strategic attacks.

The authors concluded that strategic attacks by the air force would be a priority in the event of a stalemate on the ground. Air operations could also be used to prevent decimations of the ground forces or to force a decision. Strategic bombing might also take place after the decisive battle or when there was no alternative.[28]

The War Ministry did not initially acknowledge the Luftwaffe's vision of a strategic mission. In its *Wehrmachtstudie* 1935-1936, it envisioned an air superiority role for the air force with a secondary role of army attack. In a war against France or Czechoslovakia, the air force would strike first against air bases and army lines of communication. Later it did approve the Luftwaffe's strategic thinking and force composition in its April 1938 study, *Die Kriegfuhrung als Problem der Organisation*. In this study it supported a two-step strategy of attacking the enemy's air force first, followed by raids against its economic production.[29]

The Conduct of the Air War reflected attitudes held by Wever and other air leaders toward cooperation with the army and navy. Wever had established liaison officers between air and army units. He had also urged the colocation of air division and army headquarters. Wever encouraged air force and army commanders to jointly plan and conduct command post and field exercises. These attitudes indicated an understanding of the importance of cooperation and coordination between the goals and operations of the air force with the other services.[30]

The Luftwaffe intended to fight enemy's armed forces, not its population.[31] This was consistent with the discussion in the manual concerning attacks on the enemy population centers:

> Attacks against cities made for the purpose of inducing terror in the civilian populace are to be avoided on principle. If the enemy should initiate terror attacks against defenseless and open cities, however, then retaliation attacks may be the only means of stopping the enemy from continuing this brutal method of warfare.[32]

Doctrinally, the Luftwaffe did not plan for raids on the enemy population to induce terror. It allowed that raids on populated areas for military purposes might have unintended effects and could have negative political and legal ramifications. However, it did pursue thinking into how to conduct retaliatory raids and how to defend its own cities from such raids.[33]

The Luftwaffe's plans for the opening campaign against Poland were consistent with its doctrine. The "Directive for Employment in the East" called for an "open" war with sudden powerful attacks to help the army directly and indirectly.[34] The Luftwaffe's first objective was air superiority and the destruction of the Polish Air Force, its ground organization, and the aviation industry. The secondary objective was army support involving attacks on Polish mobilization centers and cutting supply lines. The third objective included attacks on Polish military installations and armament establishments in Warsaw.[35]

Thus, the Luftwaffe developed a different idea of strategic warfare than the British. German strategic air doctrine in 1926 discussed attacks on the enemy's military, economic and moral sources of power. As the military rearmed and the Luftwaffe organization developed, its doctrine stressed strategic attacks on one source of power, the military's. German military leaders saw their primary objective as the defeat of the enemy's will to fight by defeating its armed forces through a short war. Strategic air campaigns would be useful if they promoted the German military's defeat of the enemy's armed forces; however, their utility might be limited to attacks on the enemy air force's sources of power. In the event of a stalemate between the ground forces, a strategic air campaign would become the military's main effort.

36

---

[1]Brian Bond and Williamson Murray, "The British Armed Forces, 1918-1939," in *Military Effectiveness,* vol. 2*, The Interwar Period,* eds. Allan R. Millett and Williamson Murray (Winchester, MA: Unwin Hyman, Inc., 1988), 112-113.

[2]Ministry of Defence, Directorate of Air Staff, *British Air Power Doctrine AP 3000* (London: Her Majesty's Stationery Office, 1999), 3.12.4; and Phillip S. Meilinger, "Trenchard, Slessor, and Royal Air Force Doctrine Before World War II," in *The Paths of Heaven: The Evolution of Airpower Theory,* ed. Phillip S. Meilinger (Maxwell Air Force Base, AL: Air University Press, 1997), 53.

[3]Meilinger, 53.

[4]Ibid., 54.

[5]Sir Charles Webster and Noble Frankland, *The Strategic Air Offensive Against Germany 1939-1945*, vol. 4 (London: Her Majesty's Stationery Office, 1961), 71-76.

[6]Meilinger, 54; and Webster and Frankland, 72.

[7]Meilinger, 54-55.

[8]Webster and Frankland, 72.

[9]Ibid., 56.

[10]Ministry of Defence, Directorate of Air Staff, *British Air Power Doctrine AP 3000,* 1999, 3.12.6.

[11]Bond and Murray, 120.

[12]Meilinger, 68.

[13]Webster and Frankland, 72.

[14]James S. Corum and Richard R. Muller, *The Luftwaffe's Way of War: German Air Force Doctrine, 1911-1945* (Baltimore, MD: The Nautical and Aviation Publishing Company of America, 1998), 93.

[15]Ibid., 93.

[16]Ibid., 103.

[17]Ibid., 103-104.

[18]Ibid., 99, 104.

[19]Richard Suchenwirth, *The Development of the German Air Force, 1919-1939* (New York: Arno Press, 1970), 167; James S. Corum, *The Luftwaffe: Creating the Operational Air War, 1918-1940* (Lawrence, KS: The University Press of Kansas, 1997), 140; and Larry H. Addington, *The Blitzkrieg Era and the German General Staff, 1865-1941* (New Brunswick, NJ: Rutgers University Press, 1971), 43.

[20]Headquarters, United States Strategic Air Forces in Europe (Rear) Office of the Historian, "Questionnaire of GAF Doctrine and Policy" Answers by GenMaj von Rohden (P.W.) and Col Kriesche (P.W.) to Questions submitted by Major Engelmen, 14 August 1945, 1. This document is available at the US Air Force Historical Research Center, Maxwell, AFB, AL.

[21]Horst Boog, "Higher Command and Leadership in the German Luftwaffe, 1935-1945," in *Airpower and Warfare,* eds. Alfred C. Hurley and Robert C. Ehrhart (Washington DC: U.S. Government Printing Office, 1979), 147.

[22]Corum and Muller, 120.

[23]Ibid., 120-121.

[24]Ibid., 131.

[25]Corum and Muller, 122-123; and Manfred Messerschmidt, "German Military Effectiveness Between 1919 and 1939," in *Military Effectiveness*, vol. 2*, The Interwar Period*; eds. Allan R. Millett and Williamson Murray (Winchester, MA: Unwin Hyman, Inc., 1988), 247.

[26]Corum and Muller, 123, 133.

[27]Corum and Muller, 123; and Edward L. Homze, *Arming the Luftwaffe* (Lincoln, NE: University of Nebraska Press, 1976), 131.

[28]Richard Suchenwirth, *The Development of the German Air Force, 1919-1939* (New York: Arno Press, 1970), 167-168; Boog, 147; and Messerschmidt, 241.

[29]Messerschmidt, 232, 241.

[30]James S. Corum, "The German Campaign in Norway 1940 as a Joint Operation," *The Journal of Strategic Studies* 21, no. 4 (December 1998): 51.

[31]Boog, 149.

[32]Corum and Muller, 141.

[33]Ibid., 121, 141-143.

[34]Messerschmidt, 242.

[35]"Questionnaire of GAF Doctrine and Policy," 5-6; International Military Tribunal, *Trial of the Major War Criminals Before the International Military Tribunal, Nuremburg 14 November 1945 - 1 October 1946*, vol. 9 (Nuremburg: International Military Tribunal, 1947), 175; and Albert Kesselring, *The Memoirs of Field Marshall Kesselring,* trans. William Kimber (Bonn: Athenaum, 1953; reprint, Novato, CA: Presidio Press, 1989), 45-47.
[36]

CHAPTER 7

CONCLUSION

After World War I, several airpower theorists advocated the offensive use of airpower to

defeat an enemy's will to resist. They shared a belief in the dominant nature of the defense in

land warfare and the ability of air warfare to create a decision without expending large numbers

of soldiers. These theorists believed that airpower represented a revolution in warfare.

Lieutenant Commander J. D. Prentice accurately summarized the two doctrinal choices

facing a German air arm in an article he wrote in 1929. In his article, two nations were at war

with each other, country Red and country Blue. Red chose to use its air force to attack Blue's

civilian infrastructure and vital centers. Blue's air force attacked Red's armies. Blue, by using its

air force to assist its mechanized army would be able to drive the Red army back. Since Prentice

assumed a mechanized army could move 100 miles per day, Blue would only require a matter of

days before Red's air force would be too far from Blue's frontier to mount attacks on Blue's

civilian vital centers. Red's air force would then be diverted to army support operations. To

Prentice, the occupation of enemy territory was the most effective way to suppress its

inhabitants.[1] While it may be a simplification to say German doctrine concentrated on attacking

the enemy's army, it did concentrate on producing a successful and decisive land offensive and

opted for a doctrine similar to Blue's method for using airpower.

During the Weimar Republic, German staff officers with World War I experience laid the

foundations for later German air doctrine. Analysis of tactical and technical developments in

foreign air forces and their applicability to German air force requirements was one significant

input to German doctrine. The clandestine staff analyzed total air warfare as outlined by Giulio

Douhet. Germany's own experience in World War I was also a significant input to later doctrine.

Germany's technical experience during World War I was known, but German leaders also knew

that the restrictions imposed under the Versailles Treaty limited their first-hand experience.[2]

German air theorists in the interwar period studied and understood the other major airpower theorists. Douhet was the most frequently quoted theorist and his writings were available in Germany in the late 1920s, as were Mitchell's and Trenchard's. German air leaders understood Douhet's emphasis on the offensive use of airpower and advocated similar positions. They also understood the environment about which Douhet spoke, Italy, with natural defensible frontiers. The independent use of an air force to achieve decisive results relied upon ensuring the territorial safety of the home nation. While the Great Britain of Hugh Trenchard and the United States of Billy Mitchell could also rely upon a relatively secure surface frontier, the same could not be said of Germany after World War I.

After World War I, a republic established after brief domestic turmoil governed Germany. France and the new states of Poland and Czechoslovakia surrounded Germany. Alliances between France and these states played a part in the development of insecurity inside Germany. The Treaty of Versailles also restricted the ability of Germany to defend its borders by outlawing ground fortifications and limiting Germany to a 100,000-man professional army. The navy was also restricted, and the air force was disbanded. Whereas Douhet envisioned the defensive use of the army and navy to protect the territorial integrity of the nations, especially the ground bases and infrastructure of the air force, while a decisive offensive air campaign was conducted, Germany had to plan another course of action. General Von Seeckt planned short, decisive ground campaigns relying on his relatively small army to prevent the mobilization of Germany's adversaries and prevent a two-front war.

Mere exposure to "modern" airpower theories like Douhet's did not ensure their adoption in Germany. German leaders like Von Seeckt and Wilberg appreciated the offensive nature of airpower and their doctrines and writings reflected that understanding. However, they also understood Germany's strategic position. They believed that a decisive ground campaign had the potential to spell Germany's defeat, as well as victory. Only the joint employment of the air force

83

and army toward the defeat of the enemy's most immediate threat, its armed forces, would properly defend Germany, as well as provide the key to defeating the enemy. They viewed airpower as an evolution to military theory that should be used to implement military concepts consistent with traditional German thought. One can conclude from this study that a new theory, such as the strategic use of airpower, must do more than promise a new way to defeat an abstract enemy. It must make sense, given one's specific security environment.

A nation's perceived threats also inevitably influence the development of force structure and equipment to implement doctrine, as does resource availability. Disarmament restricted German airpower during the interwar period until 1935. Throughout this period, France, Poland, and Czechoslovakia were the most probable enemies. To attack strategic targets within these nations, twin-engine and single-engine aircraft would be sufficient. If, as Wever believed, the enemies were to be the Soviet Union and Great Britain, four-engine bombers with longer ranges and payload were required. Germany's period of disarmament had limited its ability to produce large numbers of heavy bombers, so it was limited to a force suitable to support a joint campaign against nations close to German bases, like its neighboring nations. The ultimate failure of German airpower in World War II can be attributed in part to the enormous expansion of military objectives beyond those planned for and resourced in the 1930s.

Consistent leadership is also necessary to establish a new doctrine, especially one so revolutionary as independent strategic air warfare. Hugh Trenchard was Chief of the Air Staff for ten years and influential for over ten years afterward. His consistent support for the independent offensive use of airpower was reflected in the RAF's doctrine and in the teachings at the RAF staff college.

By contrast, disarmament produced a break in German air leadership. Although General von Seeckt and Major Wilberg, among others, continued to study airpower and training and plan for the future use of German airpower, there was little senior level leadership until Hermann

Goering became Air Minister. Goering and Milch had many organizational and leadership tasks that overshadowed doctrinal development. Wever and Wilberg were behind the major doctrinal pieces for the Luftwaffe, *Directives for the Execution of the Operational Air War* and *The Conduct of the Aerial War*. These documents gave credence to the strategic use of airpower to defeat the enemy military, but within a joint framework. However, their ideas on how to execute the air war were not shared by a preponderance of Luftwaffe leadership. When Kesselring and other leaders succeeded Wever, the joint use of airpower in pursuit of a decisive ground battle was given even more emphasis. This emphasis was also reflected in aircraft production choices. More consistent leadership would have contributed to a wider understanding of Hitler's strategic objectives, something Wever understood better than his successors. Luftwaffe leadership could then have concentrated on a doctrine and force structure better suited to these wider objectives. The earlier availability of an air staff college and an airpower advocate in a secure leadership position, similar to General von Seeckt's seven years in office, would have also contributed to strengthening the strategic air doctrine illustrated by the *Directives for the Execution of the Operational Air War* in 1926.

Examining the RAF and Luftwaffe's experience with doctrinal development leads to some conclusions about the role of leadership in the adoption of a revolutionary doctrine. A leader should use all the tools featured by military organizations, including staff colleges and doctrinal manuals. Staff colleges can help indoctrinate mid-level officers in a new doctrine and define an organization's accepted concepts for warfare. A senior leader with enough job security can directly effect changes to doctrine manuals. Adoption of a new doctrine also requires the leadership to take a long-term view to its organizational problems, similar to Trenchard's many years in office.

German air doctrine emphasized strategic elements of airpower more heavily in 1926 than in 1935. Its lack of professional academic study induced by the lack of an air staff college and its lack of a senior advocate for airpower contributed to the dilution of its earlier emphasis on the joint use of strategic airpower.

German air doctrine envisioned a joint use of airpower in pursuit of joint objectives, primarily the expected decisive ground campaigns to defeat enemies quickly before a feared two-front war could develop. A supporting objective for the air force and army was the prevention of the enemy from mobilizing its forces. Defeat of the enemy air force was paramount. Attacking objectives that supported the ground battle was second. Attacks on the enemy military sources of power were also part of doctrine, but definitely of secondary importance, unless the ground forces were unsuccessful or could not engage the enemy's army. This doctrine was a rational expression of Germany's plan to fight against the expected adversaries throughout much of the 1920s and 1930s, France, Czechoslovakia, and Poland. It was also demonstrably successful in 1939 and 1940.

Germany's air doctrine was not optimum against nations such as the Soviet Union and Great Britain. It was not configured to attack these enemy's sources of military power. In the case of Great Britain, the ground forces were unable to decisively engage the British forces, except during the Battle of France. Luftwaffe doctrine and force structure were unable to pursue successfully either air superiority over Great Britain or win an independent victory. In the case of the Soviet Union, the German army was unable to decisively defeat the Soviet army. Soviet military sources of power were largely beyond the reach of the Luftwaffe. A majority of German leaders did not consider the Soviet Union or Great Britain as probable enemies until the late 1930s. German industry was also unable to design and produce sufficient numbers of long-range fighters and bombers with which to win air superiority battles and attack sources of power. The inability of the German leadership to understand the mismatch of its doctrine and equipment compared to the strengths of Great Britain and the Soviet Union contributed to its failure. The fault here should be attributed to national leadership, not to the military instruments. The national leadership is responsible for ensuring the means of strategy are equal to or less than the desired ends.

Great Britain's air doctrine shifted from cooperation with the army during World War I and in 1922 to independent use as the probability of its ground forces engaging the enemy became more remote. Given its defensive situation and ability to engage in economic warfare, its doctrine appeared to be a rational use of British strengths to deter war. However, its inability to consider the means by which it would prosecute an air war if its ground forces were engaged left it with holes in its doctrine when war began. The RAF oriented its doctrine toward the kind of war it wanted to fight, and not the kind of war that would be the most dangerous for Great Britain, a war in which its army would be engaged in Continental Europe. Thus, although in a different manner form Germany, Great Britain failed to align means and ends.

The probability of a nation's ground forces to be decisively engaged appears to be inversely proportional to its desire to emphasize the strategic use of its airpower. During World War I, when Trenchard commanded British air force in France, he was more sensitive to the needs of the British ground forces under General Haig than he was to attacks on German strategic targets. RAF doctrine in 1922 also called for cooperation with the ground forces. Later, when the desirability for the British to engage in land warfare decreased, RAF doctrine stressed strategic attacks predominantly. In late 1940, when the British ground forces could not decisively engage the enemy, the RAF's strategic air campaigns became the main effort. Similarly, in 1926, German air doctrine emphasized strategic attacks more than in 1935, when Germany began to more seriously discuss how best to use its combined forces in war.

The RAF stressed the use of an independent strategic air campaign to defeat the enemy without risking a large number of ground casualties. It is reasonable, then, to assume that strategic airpower will continue to appeal to national leaders and strategists, given the present-day climate of risk-aversion. The US today is more like Great Britain than Germany. American air

87

doctrine emphasizes the use of technology to minimize ground combat. Nonetheless, Germany

provides an illuminating case study, because it instead focused on decisive ground combat

operations. Its decision-making not only contrasts with American decisions, but perhaps also

provides insights for future adversaries.

3

---

[1]J. D. Prentice, "Aircraft in War in Ten Years Time," *Journal of the Royal United Service Institution* 74, no. 496 (November 1929): 711.

[2]Wilhelm Speidel, "The Reichswehr's Illegal Air Force Command and its Secret Collaboration with Soviet Russia Before 1933," in *World War II German Military Studies,* vol. 23, eds. Donald S. Detwiler, Charles B. Burdick, and Jurgen Rohwer (New York: Garland Publishing, Inc., 1979), 23, 27, 41.

3

GLOSSARY

Heer.   Army, after 1933.

Kriegsmarine.   Navy.

Luftkriegfuhrung.   Conduct of the Air War, basic *Luftwaffe* doctrinal manual.

Luftstreitkrafte.   German Army Air Service during World War I.

Luftwaffe.   Air Force after 1933.

Luftwaffe Dienstvorschrift 16, Luftkriegfuhrung (1935).   Luftwaffe Regulation 16: The Conduct of the Aerial War.

Reichswehr.   German Armed Forces, post-World War I until 1933.

Reichsluftministerium (RLM).   Reich Air Ministry.

Reichswehrministerium (RWM).   Reich War Ministry.

Truppenamt.   Troops Office, post-World War I clandestine German General Staff.

Wehrmacht.   German Armed Forces after 1933.

.

1

1

BIBLIOGRAPHY

Books

Addington, Larry H. *The Blitzkrieg Era and the German General Staff, 1865-1941*. New Brunswick, NJ: Rutgers University Press, 1971.

Baumbach, Werner. *The Life and Death of the Luftwaffe*. Translated by Frederick Holt. New York: Ballantine Books, 1949.

Boog, Horst, ed. *The Conduct of the Air War in the Second World War*. New York: Berg Publishers, 1992.

Boyle, Andrew. *Trenchard*. New York: W.W. Norton & Company, Inc., 1962.

Cooper, Matthew. *The German Air Force, 1933-1945: An Anatomy of Failure*. London: Jane's Publishing Company Ltd., 1981.

Corum, James S. *The Roots of Blitzkrieg: Hans von Seeckt and German Military Reform*. Lawrence, KS: The University Press of Kansas, 1992.

_____. *The Luftwaffe: Creating the Operational Air War, 1918-1940*. Lawrence, KS: The University Press of Kansas, 1997.

Corum, James S., and Richard R. Muller. *The Luftwaffe's Way of War: German Air Force Doctrine 1911-1945*. Baltimore, MD: The Nautical and Aviation Publishing Company of America, 1998.

Craven, Wesley and James Lea Cate. *The Army Air Forces in World War II*, vol. 1. Chicago: University of Chicago Press, 1948.

Deighton, Len. *Fighter: The True Story of the Battle of Britain*. New York: Harper Collins Publishers, 1977.

Deighton, Len. *Blitzkrieg: From the Rise of Hitler to the Fall of Dunkirk*. New York: Harper Collins Publishers, 1977.

Deist, Wilhelm. *The Wehrmacht and German Rearmament*. Buffalo: University of Toronto Press, 1981.

Divine, David. *The Broken Wing: A Study in the British Exercise of Air Power*. London: Hutchinson and Co., 1966.

Douhet, Giulio. *The Command of the Air*. Translated by Dino Ferrari. New York: Coward-McCann, 1942. Reprint, Washington DC: Office of Air Force History, 1983.

Earle, Edward Mead, ed. *Makers of Modern Strategy: Military Thought from Machiavelli to Hitler*. Princeton, NJ: Princeton University Press, 1943. Reprint, Princeton, NJ: Princeton University Press, 1971.

Emme, Eugene M. ed. *The Impact of Air Power*. Princeton, NJ: D. Van Nostrand Company, Inc., 1959.

Fredette, Raymond H. *The Sky on Fire: The First Battle of Britain, 1917-1918, and the Birth of the Royal Air Force*. New York: Harcourt Brace Jovanovich, 1976. Reprint, Washington, DC: Smithsonian Institution Press, 1991.

Futrell, Robert Frank. *Ideas, Concepts, Doctrine: Basic Thinking in the United States Air Force 1907-1960*. Maxwell Air Force Base, Alabama: Air University Press, 1989.

Goerlitz, Walter. *History of the German General Staff 1657-1945*. Translated by Brian Battershaw. New York: Frederick A. Praeger, Inc., 1953.

Hermann, Hauptmann. *The Luftwaffe: Its Rise and Fall*. New York: G. P. Putnam's Sons, 1943.

Homze, Edward L. *Arming the Luftwaffe*. Lincoln, NE: University of Nebraska Press, 1976.

Hough, Richard, and Denis Richards. *The Battle of Britain: The Greatest Air Battle of World War II*. New York: W. W. Norton and Company, 1990.

Hoyt, Edwin P. *Angels of Death: Goering's Luftwaffe*. New York: Tom Doherty Associates, Inc., 1994.

Hurley, Alfred C., and Robert C. Ehrhart. eds. *Air Power and Warfare*. Washington, DC: U.S. Government Printing Office, 1979.

International Military Tribunal. *Trial of the Major War Criminals Before the International Military Tribunal, Nuremburg 14 November 1945 - 1 October 1946*, vol. 9. Nuremburg: International Military Tribunal, 1947.

Irving, David. *Goering: A Biography*. New York: Avon Books, 1989.

Irving, David. *The Rise and Fall of the Luftwaffe: The Life of Field Marshal Erhard Milch*. Boston: Little, Brown and Company, 1973.

Keegan, John. *The Second World War*. New York: Penguin Books, 1989.

Kennett, Lee. *A History of Strategic Bombing*. New York: Charles Scribner's Sons, 1982.

Kesselring, Albert. *The Memoirs of Field Marshall Kesselring*. Translated by William Kimber Ltd. Bonn: Athenaum, 1953. Reprint, Novato, CA: Presidio Press, 1989.

Lee, Asher. *The German Air Force*. New York: Harper and Brothers Publishers, 1946.

Macksey, Kenneth. *Kesselring: The Making of the Luftwaffe*. New York: David McKay Company, Inc., 1978.

Maier, Klaus A. "Total War and German Air Doctrine Before the Second World War" In *The German Military in the Age of Total War*, edited by Wilhelm Deist, 210-219. Dover, NH: Berg Publishers, Ltd., 1985.

Mason Jr., Herbert Molloy. *The Rise of the Luftwaffe: Forging the Secret German Air Weapon 1918-1940*. New York: Dial Press, 1973.

Meilinger, Phillip S., ed. *The Paths of Heaven: The Evolution of Airpower Theory*. Maxwell Air Force Base, AL: Air University Press, 1997.

Mets, David R. *The Air Campaign: John Warden and the Classic Airpower Theorists*. Maxwell Air Force Base, AL: Air University Press, 1999.

Millett, Alan R., and Williamson Murray. eds. *Military Effectiveness* vol. 2, *The Interwar Period*. Winchester, MA: Unwin Hyman, Inc., 1988.

Mitcham Jr., Samuel W. *Eagles of the Third Reich*. Novato, CA: Presidio Press, 1988.

Mitchell, William. *Winged Defense: The Development and Possibilities of Modern Air Power, Economic and Military*. New York: G. P. Putnam's Sons, 1925.

Muller, Richard. *The German Air War in Russia*. Baltimore, MD: The Nautical and Aviation Publishing Company of America, 1992.

Murray, Williamson. *Strategy for Defeat, The Luftwaffe, 1933–1945*. Maxwell AFB, AL: Air University Press, 1983.

_____. *The Change in the European Balance of Power, 1938-1939*. Princeton, NJ: Princeton University Press, 1984.

Murray, Williamson, and Allan R. Millett. eds. *Military Innovation in the Interwar Period.* Cambridge: Press Syndicate of the University of Cambridge, 1996.

Nielsen, Andreas. *The German Air Force General Staff.* New York: Arno Press, 1968.

Overy, Richard J. "Strategic Bombardment before 1939: Doctrine, Planning, and Operations" In C*ase Studies in Strategic Bombardment,* edited by R. Cargill Hall, 11-90. Washington, DC: U.S. Government Printing Office, 1998.

Posen, Barry R. *The Sources of Military Doctrine.* Ithaca, NY: Cornell University Press, 1984.

Price, Alfred. *Luftwaffe, Birth, Life and Death of an Air Force.* New York: Ballantine Books, 1969.

Proctor, Raymond L. *Hitler's Luftwaffe in the Spanish Civil War.* Westport, CT: Greenwood Press, 1983.

Ruge, Friedrich. *Der Seekrieg: The German Navy's Story, 1939-1945.* Annapolis, MD: United States Naval Institute, 1957.

Schliephake, Hanfried. *The Birth of the Luftwaffe.* London: Ian Allen Ltd., 1971.

Seeckt, General von. *Thoughts of a Soldier.* Translated by Gilbert Waterhouse. London: Ernest Benn Limited, 1930.

Speidel, Wilhelm. "The Reichswehr's Illegal Air Force Command and its Secret Collaboration with Soviet Russia Before 1933." In *World War II German Military Studies,* vol. 23, edited by Donald S. Detwiler, Charles B. Burdick, and Jurgen Rohwer, 1-151. New York: Garland Publishing, Inc., 1979.

Suchenwirth, Richard. *Historical Turning Points in the German Air Force War Effort.* New York: Arno Press, 1968.

Suchenwirth, Richard. *Command and Leadership in the German Air Force.* New York: Arno Press, 1970.

Suchenwirth, Richard. *The Development of the German Air Force, 1919-1939.* New York: Arno Press, 1970.

Taylor, Telford. *Sword and Swastika: Generals and Nazis in the Third Reich.* New York: Simon and Schuster, 1952.

_____. *The March of Conquest: The German Victories in Western Europe, 1940.* New York: Simon and Schuster, 1958.

Terraine, John. *The Right of the Line: The Royal Air Force in the European War 1939-1945*. Hertfordshire, UK: Wordsworth Editions Limited, 1997.

Townsend, Peter. *Duel of Eagles*. New York: Pocket Books, 1972.

Webster, Sir Charles, and Noble Frankland. *The Strategic Air Offensive Against Germany, 1939-1945*. vols. 1 and 4. London: Her Majesty's Stationery Office, 1961.

Wheeler-Bennett, John W. *The Nemesis of Power: The German Army in Politics, 1918-1945*. London: Macmillan & Co. Ltd., 1953.

Periodicals And Articles

Corum, James S. "The Old Eagle as Phoenix: The Luftstreitkrafte Creates an Operational Air War Doctrine, 1919-1920," *Air Power History* 39, no. 1 (spring 1997): 13-21.

_____. "The Development of Strategic Air War Concepts in Interwar Germany, 1919-1939." *Air Power History* 44, no. 4 (winter 1997): 18-35.

_____. "The German Campaign in Norway 1940 as a Joint Operation." *The Journal of Strategic Studies* 21, no. 4 (December 1998): 50-77.

Ehrhart, Robert C. "Some Thoughts on Air Force Doctrine." *Air University Review* 31, no. 3 (1980): 29-38.

English, Allan D. "The RAF Staff College and the Evolution of Strategic Bombing Policy, 1922-1929." *The Journal of Strategic Studies* 16, no. 3 (September 1993): 408-431.

Ferris, John. "The Theory of a 'French Air Menace', Anglo-French Relations and the British Home Defense Air Force Programmes of 1921-25." *The Journal of Strategic Studies* 10, no. 1 (March 1997): 62-83.

Galland, Adolf. "Defeat of the *Luftwaffe*: Fundamental Causes." *Air University Quarterly Review* 6, no.1 (spring 1953): 18-36.

Gray, Peter W. "The Battle of Britain." *Royal Air Force Air Power Review* 3, no. 3 (2000): 16-32.

Homze, Edward L. "The Luftwaffe's Failure to Develop a Heavy Bomber Before World War II." *Aerospace Historian* 24, no. 1 (March 1977): 20-26.

Meilinger, Phillip S. "Trenchard and 'Morale Bombing': The Evolution of Royal Air Force Doctrine Before World War II." *The Journal of Military History* 60 (April 1996): 243-270.

Murray, Williamson. "British and German Air Doctrine Between the Wars." *Air University Review* 31, no. 3 (1980): 39-58.

_____. "The *Luftwaffe* Before the Second World War: A Mission, A Strategy?" *The Journal of Strategic Studies 4*, no. 3 (September 1981): 261-270.

Overy, Richard. J. "Hitler and Air Strategy." *Journal of Contemporary History* 15 (1980): 405-421.

_____. "Doctrine not Dogma: Lessons From the Past." *The Royal Air Force Air Power Review* 3, no. 1 (spring 2000): 32-46.

Prentice, J. D. "Aircraft in War in Ten Years Time." *Journal of the Royal United Service Institution* 74, no. 496 (November 1929): 705-713.

Segre, Claudio. "Douhet in Italy: Prophet Without Honor?" *Aerospace Historian* 26 (June 1979): 69-80.

Government Documents

US Air Force. Air Force Doctrine Document 1*: Air Force Basic Doctrine.* Washington, DC: U.S. Government Printing Office, September 1997.

Chairman of the Joint Chiefs of Staff. Joint Pub 1-02, *Department of Defense Dictionary of Military and Associated Terms.* Washington, DC: U.S. Government Printing Office, 23 March 1994, amended 6 April 1999.

United Kingdom. Ministry of Defence. Directorate of Air Staff. *British Air Power Doctrine AP 3000.* London: Her Majesty's Stationery Office, 1999.

Unpublished Materials

Headquarters Air P/W Interrogation Detachment, Military Intelligence Service, 9th Air Force. *Enemy Intelligence Summaries, Hermann Goering.* Military Intelligence Service, 9th US Air Force. 1 June 1945.

Headquarters, United States Strategic Air Forces in Europe (Rear) Office of the Historian, "Questionnaire of GAF Doctrine and Policy" Answers by GenMaj von Rohden (P.W.) and Col Kriesche (P.W.) to Questions submitted by Major

Engelmen, 14 Aug 1945. United States Air Force Historical Research Center, Maxwell AFB (USAFHRC) 519.619.7 p.1

OKC, Generalstab 8, Abteilung, 22.11.1944, "The Douhet Theory and its Application to the Present War." Air Historical Branch Translation No. VII/11, USAFHRC 512.621 VII/11.

Other Sources

Cappelluti, Frank Joseph. "The Life and Thoughts of Giulio Douhet." Ph.D. diss., Rutgers University, 1967.

Thoeny, Alan Robert. "Role of the Separate Air Force in Nazi Germany." Thesis, University of Wisconsin, 1963.

1

_____

INITIAL DISTRIBUTION LIST

1. Combined Arms Research Library
   U.S. Army Command and General Staff College
   250 Gibbon Ave.
   Fort Leavenworth, KS 66027-2314

2. Defense Technical Information Center/OCA
   8725 John J. Kingman Rd., Suite 944
   Fort Belvoir, VA 22060-6218

3. Naval War College Library
   Hewitt Hall
   U.S. Navy War College
   Newport, RI 02841-5010

4. Dr. Christopher R. Gabel
   Combat Studies Institute
   USACGSC
   1 Reynolds Ave.
   Fort Leavenworth, KS 66027-1352

5. CDR John T. Kuehn
   Navy Element
   USACGSC
   1 Reynolds Ave.
   Fort Leavenworth, KS 66027-1352

6. Major Robert J. Dague
   Air Force Element
   USACGSC
   1 Reynolds Ave.
   Fort Leavenworth, KS 66027-1352

CERTIFICATION FOR MMAS DISTRIBUTION STATEMENT

1. <u>Certification Date</u>:   <u>1 June 2001</u>

2. <u>Thesis Author</u>:   <u>LCDR William R. Muscha</u>

3. <u>Thesis Title</u>:   <u>Strategic Airpower Elements in Interwar German Air Force Doctrine</u>

    _____

4. <u>Thesis Committee Members</u>   _____
       <u>Signatures</u>:   _____

                                          _____

5. <u>Distribution Statement</u>: See distribution statements A-X on reverse, then circle appropriate distribution statement letter code below:

         A   B   C   D   E   F   X   SEE EXPLANATION OF CODES ON REVERSE

If your thesis does not fit into any of the above categories or is classified, you must coordinate with the classified section at CARL.

6. <u>Justification</u>: Justification is required for any distribution other than described in Distribution on Statement A. All or part of a thesis may justify distribution limitation. See limitation justification statements 1-10 on reverse, then list, below, the statement(s) that applies (apply) to your thesis and corresponding chapters/sections and pages. Follow the example format shown below:

EXAMPLE

<u>Limitation Justification Statement</u>		<u>Chapter/Section</u>		<u>Page(s)</u>
<u>Direct Military Support (10)</u>	/	<u>Chapter 3</u>	/	<u>12</u>
<u>Critical Technology (3)</u>	/	<u>Section 4</u>	/	<u>31</u>
<u>Administrative Operational Use (7)</u>	/	<u>Chapter 2</u>	/	<u>13-32</u>

Fill in limitation justification for your thesis below:

<u>Limitation Justification Statement</u>	<u>Chapter/Section</u>	<u>Page(s)</u>
_____ /	_____ /	_____

7. <u>MMAS Thesis Author's Signature</u>:   _____

STATEMENT A: Approved for public release; distribution is unlimited. (Documents with this statement may be made available or sold to the general public and foreign nationals.)

STATEMENT B: Distribution authorized to US Government agencies only (insert reason and date ON REVERSE OF THIS FORM). Currently used reasons for imposing this statement include the following:

    1. Foreign Government Information. Protection of foreign information.

    2. Proprietary Information. Protection of proprietary information not owned by the US Government.

    3. Critical Technology. Protection and control of critical technology including technical data with potential military application.

    4. Test and Evaluation. Protection of test and evaluation of commercial production or military hardware.

    5. Contractor Performance Evaluation. Protection of information involving contractor performance evaluation.

    6. Premature Dissemination. Protection of information involving systems or hardware from premature dissemination.

    7. Administrative/Operational Use. Protection of information involving restricted to official use or for administrative or operational purposes.

    8. Software Documentation. Protection of software documentation--release only in accordance with the provisions of DoD Instruction 7930.2.

    9. Specific Authority: Protection of information required by a specific authority.

    10. Direct Military Support. To protect export-controlled technical data of such military significance that release for purposes other than direct support of DoD-approved activities may jeopardize a U.S. military advantage.

STATEMENT C: Distribution authorized to U.S. Government agencies and their contractors: (REASON AND DATE). Currently most used reasons are 1, 3, 7, 8, and 9 above.

STATEMENT D: Distribution authorized to DoD and U.S. DoD contractors only: (REASON AND DATE). Currently most used reasons are 1, 3, 7, 8, and 9 above.

STATEMENT E: Distribution authorized to DoD only; (REASON AND DATE). Currently most used reasons are 1, 2, 3, 4, 5, 6, 7, 8, 9, and 10.

STATEMENT F: Further dissemination only as directed by (controlling DoD office and date), or higher DoD authority. Used when the DoD originator determines that information is subject to special dissemination limitation specified by paragraph 4-505, DoD 5200.1-R.

STATEMENT X: Distribution authorized to US Government agencies and private individuals of enterprises eligible to obtain export-controlled technical data in accordance with DoD Directive 5230.25; (date). Controlling DoD office is (insert).

www.ingramcontent.com/pod-product-compliance
Lightning Source LLC
Chambersburg PA
CBHW081338090426
42737CB00017B/3204